COMMUNICATING
WITH
THE JAPANESE

COMMUNICATING
WITH
THE JAPANESE

J. V. Neustupný

THE JAPAN TIMES
TOKYO, JAPAN
1987

First edition, November 1987
Fourth printing, June 1990
All rights reserved.
Copyright © 1987 by J.V. Neustupný.
Cover art by Kazuyuki Sasaki, Horinsha, Inc.
Book design, typography, and editorial supervision
by Stephen Comee.
This book may not be reproduced in whole or in part, by photocopy, mimeograph, or any
other means, without permission.
For information, write: The Japan Times, Ltd.,
5-4 Shibaura 4-chome, Minato-ku, Tokyo 108, Japan.

ISBN 4-7890-0364-7

Published in Japan by The Japan Times, Ltd.

This book and many other fine books on Japan and the Japanese culture and language are
edited, designed, and published by and for The Japan Times, Ltd., at its main office, located at
5-4 Shibaura 4-chome, Minato-ku,
Tokyo 108, Japan.

PRINTED IN JAPAN

CONTENTS

PREFACE

From this book a start can be made in many directions. It is addressed to all those who face the problem of communication with the Japanese through the medium of either English or Japanese. They may be tourists, short term visitors or residents, business people meeting their Japanese contacts, people in international organizations whose colleagues are Japanese, or simply those who are about to embark on a Japanese language course, in Japan or overseas. The book will be of use to all these categories of readers. It should help some to understand their hosts or guests, neighbors or friends, and work contacts; some to spend happier days in Japan; and others simply to learn the language more efficiently.

As Japan's economic power has continued growing through the 1980s, the attitudes of some sections of Western societies to Japan have started changing. The honeymoon of the 1960s and 1970s is over. With conflict in the economic sphere, overt or latent, problems of understanding and communication have moved to the foreground. More than ever we now need to know who the Japanese are, and how to communicate with them.

One of the most important tasks in the new phase of our relationship with Japan is not to let problems in economic interaction introduce an unwanted bias into our understanding of Japan and our individual relationships with the Japanese. For this purpose it is essential that we not only understand the nature of the economic arguments concerned and the relations at the level of corporations and governments, but also problems in communication between individuals.

In this book I have attempted to show what such problems of communication between individuals are. I have also listed a number of points that we should know if we want to successfully interact. I firmly believe that the Japanese are not so different, not so "typically Japanese" as many suggest. More than often the assumed differences are only due to our inability to communicate. The reader will find that I do not side with any quick and extreme interpretation of Japan. I do not attempt to explain the whole of Japan by a single simple formula. The Japanese will neither be idealized — in the style of the 1970s — nor accused of mystical nationalism or similar vices — as at the end of the 1980s. Realism is what is needed. Those who have discovered in Japan the ultimate model of the future of mankind will not like this book. Neither will those for whom the Japanese are a priori inscrutable, unfriendly, and untrustworthy. The real Japan is neither of these extremes.

Readers should realize that this book is not an introduction to facts about Japan, Japanese communication, or Japanese language. Although many facts are quoted, the emphasis is on the more general problem of understanding. Those interested in the amount of the GNP, a listing of political parties, the names of newspapers, or an explanation of what Kabuki is should see other publications which range in extent from the simple *Japan—An International Comparison,* published by the Keizai Koho Center to the nine volumes of Kodansha's *Encyclopedia of Japan.* In between there is a whole sea of literature about Japan in general and about its individual aspects. Some interpretations in such publications may of course differ from those offered in this book. It will not be necessary to emphasize that the view of Japan embodied in the following text is not the ultimate truth. Readers will be able to compare it with other sources and their own experience, and arrive at their own conclusions.

Jiří V. Neustupný

ACKNOWLEDGMENTS

I wish to acknowledge the assistance of a number of institutions and individuals without which this book could not have been written.

The Australia-Japan Foundation and its Executive Director Mr. Peter Hocker showed great understanding at the outset of this project and supported my work throughout. Much of the data was collected and checked when I was in Tokyo in 1982 as a Japan Foundation Fellow. However, the manuscript could not have been completed without the opportunity of three months of concentrated work at the Institute of Culture and Communication of the East-West Center in Honolulu from April to June 1986.

I owe much to the seminal atmosphere of the Japanese Studies Centre in Melbourne and the Department of Japanese at Monash University. Comments on sections of the manuscript of this book were received in particular from Dr. Anthony Backhouse, Ms. Robyn Spence-Brown, Dr. Akito Ozaki, and Dr. Yutaka Yamada. Ms. Helen Marriott, Ms. Reiko Neustupný and Dr. Yoshio Sugimoto read virtually the whole first draft of my manuscript and supplied a large number of extremely useful comments. Any reader who has a serious interest in the sociology of Japan will easily recognize areas of contact between this book and Mouer and Sugimoto's *Images of Japanese Society* (Routledge & Kegan Paul) which I consider to be the best introduction to the understanding of Japan ever written by sociologists.

In Honolulu, Dr. Wimal Dissanayake, Ms. Sharon Mann, and Dr. Björn Jernudd provided invaluable advice. Dr. Jernudd in particular helped with both planning and wording of the entire first draft. In addition, I also acknowledge with deep gratitude the assistance of Professor Florian Coulmas of the University of Düsseldorf; Professor Nozomu Kawamura of the Department of Sociology, Tokyo Municipal University; Professor Fujio Minami of the National Language Research Institute in Tokyo; and Mr. Daisuke Nishimura of NHK (Japan Broadcasting Corp.). Each of them kindly checked the text of a chapter of this book. It goes without saying that all responsibility for errors or misinterpretations remains entirely with the author.

Finally, I must thank Mr. Masayuki Ishida of the *Japan Times* for his patience in waiting for the manuscript and Mr. Stephen Comee for carefully editing and designing this book. Any book is the product of cooperation between the author and the publisher. I have indeed been very fortunate to be able to cooperate on this manuscript with the *Japan Times*.

Readers who wish to furnish comments are welcome to write to the following address: Professor J. V. Neustupný, Department of Japanese, Monash University, Clayton, Victoria 3168, Australia.

Jiří V. Neustupný

COMMUNICATING
WITH
THE JAPANESE

ONE
THE PROBLEM OF
COMMUNICATION

To communicate is an exciting experience. Thus, communication with the Japanese is not always a "problem." Many people succeed, deriving both spiritual and material profit and pleasure from it.

Communicating with the Japanese opens doors to one of the technically most advanced civilizations of the world. It also leads to the appreciation of a great and unique culture which possesses considerable potential for contributing to world culture in a significant way. In addition, the Japanese people are not merely polite, they are also friendly, sincere, and honest — like any other people in the world. The Japanese scenery has justly been described as among the most beautiful in the world. To travel or to live in Japan provides most foreigners with memories lasting for life.

Of course, Japan is only one of many settings for communication with the Japanese. In the internationalized society of the last decades of the twentieth century increasing numbers of the Japanese live and work overseas. They become neighbors who live across the street and colleagues whose work place is the same as ours. Their children go to school with our children.

When one speaks about the "problems of communication," reference is made to a number of those foreigners who did not quite succeed. That such people exist should not surprise. Communication across cultural boundaries is always difficult. Misunderstandings occur even among close allies and Japan, though not exotic or vastly different, is more different for most foreigners than any of their neighbors. Although many other Asian societies are quickly catching up, Japanese society is still the only highly industrialized and modern society in the world which has a fully developed culture based on other than Western foundations. This fact, though rendering communication difficult, makes Japan even more attractive. In this country, perhaps, alternative solutions can be found for issues we face in our own societies.

HOW TO COMMUNICATE

One of the most widely distributed superstitions about communication is that its sole prerequisite is what we call ''language.'' Language teachers and those who engage in the study of grammars have played a particularly active role in spreading this myth. Of course, there should be no doubt that ''language'' (in the sense of grammar, vocabulary, pronunciation, and script) does play an important part. However, if we want to communicate, we must know more than language. In the first instance, it is necessary to master rules of communication other than those that are normally included in the language teacher's usage of the word. For instance, we cannot speak unless we know whom we are allowed to address, what we are allowed to say, whether and how to support our speech by gestures, and many other things. In other words, not only *linguistic* but also *communicative* competence is necessary.

Secondly, we must possess an adequate understanding of the people with whom we are communicating. One cannot successfully communicate with somebody one knows nothing about. What aims do our communication partners put before themselves, what do they think about the issues to be discussed, how does their family or professional life influence their thought and their communication? We can call knowledge of this type *cultural* competence. Communication is unthinkable not only without linguistic, but also without communicative and cultural competence. This book will attempt to provide an introduction to all these three types of knowledge necessary for communication.

Cultural Competence

Culture includes communication and communication includes

language. However, what we have in mind here are those components of culture that are not primarily designed as vehicles of communication: patterns of thought, conduct of daily life, the arts, and all that is included in the everyday use of the word "culture."

When, before dinner, you discussed business matters with Mr. Nakamura, you had, of course, no doubt that without detailed knowledge of the aims and current demands of your company and without the knowledge of Mr. Nakamura's business situation and aspirations you would be unable to get anywhere. Yet, when it comes to personal communication, some foreign speakers assume that they can manage with simply knowing how to produce sentences, without understanding the particular social and cultural circumstances of the people they are communicating with.

Communicative and cultural behavior are intricately chained together. One has to know the topography of the place and the traffic system in order to get to a party, one has to know how to drink sherries (one doesn't drink sherry like one drinks beer, a point concerning which some Japanese are not absolutely sure), how to peel oranges (which many non-Japanese are not very adept at), how to play cards, and many other things. If we do not know how to perform the non-communicative acts which accompany communicative acts in daily life, such as conversation at a party, we cannot successfully communicate. Also, culture enters into communication as its topic, and someone who knows nothing about Japanese sports can only stand and listen when sports are discussed. However, the most important matter is that our partners, as members of a different culture, may think in a different way, hold different attitudes, and have different expectations. It is because of all these reasons that when studying the Japanese language, the study of the Japanese society and culture is not an additional extra but a must without which we cannot "get there."

In this book, Chapter II will elaborate on some facts of Japanese society and culture that are of particular relevance for communication with the Japanese.

Communicative Competence

As mentioned above, communicative competence is a narrower concept than cultural competence. It was developed mainly in the sociolinguistics of the 1960s and 1970s. This competence covers much more than what is called language in ordinary language text-books. As sociolinguist Dell Hymes has pointed out, without acquiring this competence, we would be like parrots who can pronounce perfect sentences, but cannot use them at the correct time, do not worry about whom they are addressing, and in general, apply sentences out of context.

Communicative competence can be classified in many ways; to further illustrate what its full range is, I shall use eight categories.

(1) *Under what conditions do we switch on communication?*

The speaker must know for what purpose and under what conditions communication takes place in Japanese. Of course, as in other languages, one mostly asks a question when information is urgently needed. But how about talking when there is little or nothing to say, as, for instance, when one meets an acquaintance at a bus stop? In many languages there is an obligation to talk. How about Japanese? Further, how about situations in which we notice considerable communicative activity in the case of Japanese speakers (note taking, diary keeping, etc.), when much more individual variation would probably appear in English.

(2) *What type of language should be used?*

Among the rules of communicative competence an important role is played by rules which determine what "type of language" (in sociolinguistics this is called "variety of language") should be used. It is not a haphazard process through which we opt for communication in Japanese or English, in the standard language or in a dialect, in a formal or informal style of speech, or in a serious or a joking tone. Under what conditions is English acceptable in Japan? Should one be rather formal? When can one be informal or even joke?

(3) *At what times and places do we communicate?*

We also must know what times and places are appropriate for communication. For instance, when visiting a Japanese home, should greetings and introductions be performed at the door or should one wait until being shown into the lounge? What is the best setting (place and time) for developing an informal cordial relationship with your Japanese contact? What, in general, are the differences between places and times appropriate for communication in Japanese and English?

(4) *Which people participate in communication?*

No communication can take place unless at least two participants agree to establish a "network." Who then can or should be addressed when we are asking in downtown Tokyo for directions to a department store? How should networks be established with people you want to befriend? It has often been asserted that Japanese society consists of very closed networks. Is this true, and if so, can foreigners ever communicate with the Japanese on an equal basis?

Problems of network establishment are fundamental in any act of communication. For learners of Japanese the establishment and maintenance of networks also means that unless they can find Japanese who agree to speak to them, there will be no practice, and no learning.

(5) *What content is communicated?*

For someone who wants to convey a message, an extremely important piece of knowledge is what should and what should not be communicated. Are there some "good" topics and some "bad" ones? Which themes, topics, or words should be avoided? How can one best communicate one's own attitudes and intentions? Are the Japanese really so polite, and how can respect be communicated? Is it true that the Japanese avoid a clear negative answer to questions?

(6) *What form do verbal messages take?*

How are messages built up from sentences? What is the form of a typical telephone message (e.g., does one start with "hello, how are you" or *konnichi wa* in Japanese), or of a letter (e.g., does a letter have the writer's address inside)? How are conversations opened, developed, and closed? How about fixed-form (routine) messages such as the famous short or extended Japanese greetings?

(7) *What channels of communication are used?*

Messages can be shaped in various media. We can also say that messages can be sent through different "channels." For instance one can use voice (the oral channel), writing (the written channel), facial expression (e.g., to express contempt or amusement by laughing), body movements, or other "non-verbal" channels. What meaning is attributed in Japanese, for instance, to various modes of laughter, ways of sitting, gestures, or to the ways we dress? This issue of "non-verbal communication" has recently attracted the attention of the general public. Obviously, it is a very important, topic, though not the only one important for the issue of communicative competence.

(8) *How do the Japanese maintain their language?*

In all systems of communication people attach various labels to various types of language, evaluate that type of language, and take measures toward its improvement. However, this "behaviour toward language," as Joshua Fishman has called it, often follows different trends in different languages. We wish to know whether there are any particular features of speech (either in Japanese or in English) that are negatively evaluated in Japanese. What mistakes should be strictly avoided? How should one correct one's own mistakes? Is it appropriate to hesitate a lot? If so, how? Is one allowed to ask a speaker to repeat what he said?

Chapter III of this book will be devoted to further detailed discussion of communicative competence necessary for interaction with the Japanese.

Linguistic Competence

The traditional "language," that is, linguistic competence, is a part of communicative competence. Language is actually a set of rules of communicative competence that enable us to construct correct sentences within communication acts. However, the generally accepted tradition is to treat language as something special. This book will acknowledge this tradition and devote to the Japanese language the whole of Chapter IV.

Linguistic competence as native speakers possess it includes the ability to code thought into appropriate words, to chain these words into grammatically correct sentences, and pronounce or write down such sentences in an acceptable manner. Even readers who do not intend to study Japanese in detail should profit from knowing some basic facts about the language.

While different from English and most other European languages,

Japanese is not vastly different: our Japanese interlocutors are not performing some exotic or unimaginable acrobatics when they speak the language. Wild speculations sometimes circulate about the polite expressions in Japanese, but the way in which they are actually used by the Japanese is absolutely different from the way in which these "honorifics" are portrayed in *The Mikado* by Gilbert and Sullivan. I shall point later in this book to the fact that the function honorifics perform in Japanese is performed by other means in other languages: the basic aim, paying respect to other speakers, is the same. I shall also explain that the Japanese writing system is different and difficult, but that there is nothing irrational or mystical about it.

An example of the usefulness of basic information about Japanese even for those who do not intend to study the language in detail is the use of such knowledge when employing interpreters. A foreigner who knows that the order of words and clauses in a Japanese sentence is often the opposite of the English order can substantially help his interpreter. One way is to construct shorter sentences. Another way is to pronounce the whole sentence as one whole, rather than to cut it into shorter segments. When a sentence is cut into short chunks the interpreter cannot work, because what comes in English in the last part of the sentence must often be put at the beginning of the sentence in Japanese.

CONTACT SITUATIONS

Apart from the three types of competence necessary for communication with the Japanese one other basic term must be explained here: "contact situation."

"Contact" (or "foreign") situation is a situation in which members of two or more cultures interact. Contact situations normally contain more than one language, more than one system of communication, and more than one culture. Situations in which foreigners interact with the Japanese are of course contact situations. On the other hand, situations of interaction between members of the same culture are "native" (or "internal") situations.

The distinction between contact and native situations is basic. We must realize that behavior in contact situations is very different from behavior in native situations. In contact situations, participants are exposed to much greater strain; they experience a much larger number of interaction, communication, and language problems. For instance, those who can speak fluently may stutter. Those who are normally polite can sound rather abrasive. People who possess a very good judgment can became indecisive. Contact situations are also characterized by constant attempts to solve language, communication, and cultural problems. All this is applicable to both the Japanese and to us.

Depending on what language is being used in a contact situation, we normally speak about ''native'' participants and ''foreign'' participants. It is a fact of life that only a very small percentage of contact situations including the Japanese is conducted in Japanese. The Japanese are normally the foreign participants. We should realize that this puts them in a disadvantaged position; much of the burden of adaptation is on them. The number of communication problems they face is much larger than what we normally experience—unless we ourselves communicate in Japanese.

However, the fact that a particular language is used does not decide everything. Even when English is employed some rules of communication and of culture can be Japanese. You may have noticed that many foreigners address the Japanese not with their first name or as Mr./Mrs./Ms. Kimura, but as Kimura-san. In other words, they accept the Japanese pattern. On the other hand, the Japanese, too, do not adapt in a perfect fashion. Even though English may be used, they may feel that they would prefer being addressed in a way that is closer to the Japanese system (e.g., Mr. Satō rather than Hiro), that topics can follow the Japanese system of topics (e.g., commencing conversation by discussing common friends), that the deportment of the participants should also be Japanese (e.g., no crossed legs in the presence of a superior), and perhaps that the meeting should take place on tatami. Of course, when the vehicle of communication is Japanese, similar adaptations occur. Foreigners are then not necesarily bound by all rules which bind the Japanese participants and they experience a number of problems which do not occur in native Japanese-to-Japanese situations.

Initially, teachers of Japanese considered that their task was to tell foreigners how the Japanese spoke among themselves and teach them to do likewise. They forgot that the students will not become fluent in the language for many years, that they will behave like typical foreign speakers, and that native speakers will not behave toward them in the same way that they behave toward other native speakers. The situations in which such learners will participate will therefore be contact, not native situations. The learners will have to acquire competence in how to handle a number of problems typical to foreigners: How to compensate for the lack of vocabulary, how to avoid certain forms, and how to listen for the correct accent and imitate it. They should know how they can slow down the tempo of speech of their Japanese partners and many other things. Foreign speakers should also be told that the language the Japanese will use to them will not necessarily be normal Japanese, and that it may be a variety of what we often call "foreigner talk." Of course, the same is true about communication and culture. Foreigners must know that many features of communication and cultural behavior of the Japanese in contact situations will simply not be the same as what they are in native situations. In this book an attempt will be made to outline what such additional knowledge should be.

Types of Communication Problems in Contact Situations

According to the most popular picture of communication problems in intercultural contact situations, people who speak a foreign language badly cannot make themselves understood. This "communication breakdown" does of course occur, but it is by far not the only type of communication problem that occurs in contact situations. An equally important problem is the case of communicating incorrectly about one's intentions or personality. There are also problems which result in the speaker's or listener's tiredness, and in a number of other effects. Let me give some examples.

(1) *Communication Breakdown*
Japanese speakers with a low degree of competence in English often cannot pronounce some words correctly. There are stories about pairs of English words distinguished by a single consonant which, mispronounced by the Japanese, caused misunderstanding or embarrassment (e.g., "rice" vs. "lice," "election" vs. "erection," etc.). However, what perhaps happens more frequently is that we simply do not undersand what the other speaker has said.

A foreign student who just arrived in Japan was shown to her room on the upper floor of Mr. Yoshida's house. She unpacked and then came down to join the others who were busy with preparing for dinner. Trying not to show how difficult it was for her to speak Japanese she turned to Mrs. Yoshida, starting her sentence *Tasukete.* . . . The whole family turned pale with fright. They rushed to the student's room, but surprisingly it was not on fire. What happened? The word *tasukete* means "help!" What the student wanted to say was *Tetsudaimashō ka?* "Can I help you?" However, she used the incorrect verb and did not finish the sentence—that would at least have made it clear for the Yoshidas that she was asking a question rather then making an appeal.

These examples of communication breakdown are due to problems in language competence. However, this does not mean that breakdown would never result from insufficient communicative or cultural competence. Many cases of misunderstanding are due to jokes, which are perfectly understood linguistically, but interpreted as serious statements. Lack of cultural knowledge may cause misunderstanding in communication, for instance, when the foreign speaker does not know much about the topic which is being discussed, say baseball. The native speaker may presuppose too much, and the result may be that the thread of discourse is cut with little possibility of joining it again.

Of course, not all cases of misunderstanding are fatal. The result may be not a complete breakdown, but simply a partial misunderstanding of the message. Many misunderstandings can be solved on the spot if the speakers know how to proceed in sorting such problems out. But this is not always easy to do in a contact situation.

Contact situations require much understanding and genuine effort from the native speaker to assist the foreign speaker with his or her problems. Not all native speakers are prepared to accept this special effort, some because of their laziness, others because they do not realize what the nature of the problem is.

(2) *Misunderstood Personality*

Native members of any culture are usually quick in connecting verbal performance of foreign speakers in contact situations with personality. One often says "He is an extrovert," or "She is so shy." The speakers concerned may not be "extroverts" or "shy" in native situations within their own culture at all. However, when communicating in a foreign language, they may be losing the ability to communicate correctly about their personality. This is a common problem and an important one. Whatever language we speak, we want to remain ourselves. However, this is often difficult to achieve.

Let us consider an Australian student studying in Japan. He is a very friendly, polite, and serious fellow. Since he speaks quite a bit of Japanese, his networks are reasonably wide. However, he is taken for a rather cheeky and unruly person. If you watch the way he communicates, you can see that from the point of view of Japanese he is too informal; he is too casually dressed even when invited by Japanese friends on a formal occasion—he thinks that to put on a clean shirt is to be dressed rather formally, he sits in a very relaxed manner, he blows his nose in front of others, and he laughs too loudly.

It is not difficult to contrast him with a Japanese student in Australia. According to his host family, Ken'ichi is always taciturn, likes to be left to himself, is rather passive. When interviewed in Japanese, he is no different from the average Japanese student in Japan. However, his rather low competence in English makes him avoid communication. According to his host family he also has some other strange "personality" features. He is very formal: whenever introduced to anyone (even to a child), he says "How do you do." Of course, this is the only English phrase for that occasion he was taught at school in Japan, but it sounds formal in Australian English. When driven to the railway station each morning by his host mother he sits in the back seat of the car. This is rude in Australia, where the meaning is "you are my chauffeur." For Ken'ichi, this means nothing at all.

Of course, I should hasten to say that thousands of foreigners do not encounter problems such as this. However, many do. Native speakers must learn how not to put labels on foreign speakers too hastily. We must distinguish real personality features from features that appear in a contact situation and are nothing else than a sign of a foreign speaker fighting with his or her own communication problems. Not many native speakers can easily make such a distinction.

(3) *Fatigue*

Another result of communication in contact situations may be that either the foreign or the native participant or both become tired. There are too many hurdles, of linguistic as well as of communicative and cultural nature, which lead to fatigue, and you may have met people who avoid foreigners because of this. Certainly a foreign speaker of Japanese in the USA (and a USA speaker of Japanese in Japan) often feel at the end of the day that they want to be left alone, rather than to be rushed into a new communicative adventure. Again the strain is more intensive for foreign than for native participants in contact situations: one must look for words, struggle in chaining them together, control one's laughter, look for conversation topics, try to remain polite, think about the cultural meaning of what has been said, and eat and perhaps sit in an unusual way. Where so many things have to be attended to, the day may be rather long. The seeming passivity of many foreign speakers and their attempt to avoid invitations to communicative encounters, such as a lunch or a party, must be seen in this context.

Again, here is a test case for native speakers. Can they understand what problems the foreign speakers face? Can they suppress the feeling of irritation which easily appears on the basis of their own discomfort in the encounter? Can they comprehend and help, not in the patronizing style of "foreigner talk," but in a more subtle and effective way?

Where Do Communication Problems Come From?

This book cannot give a full prescription that will remove all communication problems successfully. It can merely provide some basic suggestions for the reader's own treatment kit. However, for this purpose, it is necessary to add a few notes on the sources of communication problems.

(1) *Influence of the Native System*

The most popular explanation of the presence of problems in contact situations is through the influence of the speaker's native language, communication system, or culture. For instance, the usage of the verbs "to come" and "to go" is somewhat different from that of their Japanese counterparts *kuru* and *iku*. When departing with a group of friends for a movie you can ask another friend "Why don't you come along?"; however, the correct verb in Japanese is *iku* "to go." If you use *kuru*, "to come," this constitutes an error which can be attributed to the influence of English. Similarly, a Japanese may bow while saying "good morning," because to bow with any verbal greeting is the required norm in Japanese.

To give an example which concerns culture: a friend of mine believed for a long time that the Japanese go each Sunday morning for a Buddhist service. This was based on the fact that people in his home town were going to the local Catholic church each Sunday.

There is no doubt that many problems in contact situations can be explained in this way. However, in a large number of cases people make mistakes not because they implement rules of their own language, communication, and culture, but for other reasons. At least two other important factors are at work.

(2) *Interim Assumptions about the Foreign System*

The first of these two factors can be called *interim assumptions* or "approximations." While learning a new language, communication system, or culture, all learners use assumptions and approximations before they "get it right." Such assumptions are not always based on the experience of one's own language but may have been learned, such as, for instance, the image one has about foreign languages, communication, and culture in general. A frequent case is when a certain principle acquired by the learner is generalized and extended to cover all cases in which it might apply. For instance, "Jiro's car" is in Japanese *Jirō no kuruma*, but "old car" is not *furui no kuruma*, as many beginners say, but simply *furui kuruma* (without the particle *no*). The mistake is based on the wrong assumption that all modifiers preceding nouns (here: *kuruma* or "car"), are connected with the noun by the particle *no*. Obviously, this wrong assumption is not influenced by English, because in English, as in Japanese, the connection is different. In the former sentence one attaches an "'s" (as in "Jiro's"), while in the latter case there is no formal marker (as in "old"). Thus, the structure of the English expression corresponds roughly to the correct Japanese sentences.

Assumptions of this kind are called "interim" because they frequently appear at the initial stages of learning and may later be removed and replaced by correct rules. Of course, if the process of learning is not completed, such wrong assumptions frequently lose their interim status and become what language teachers call "fossilized." By the way, all errors in a foreign speaker's language may become fossilized and this is a point when no language teaching methods available at the moment can usually help any more.

Interim assumptions are made not only in the case of language, but also with regard to communication and culture. Many Japanese users of English make an incorrect assumption that everyone is addressed in English as Mr., Mrs., Ms., or Miss. However, this assumption is not true, at least not in the writer's English (a variety of Australian English), since people with titles such as Dr., Reverend, Senator, etc. are normally addressed as Dr. Smith, Reverend Miller, or Senator McDonald. On the cultural side, there is a common expectation by those who know a little about Japan that most Japanese can explain quite a lot about Zen Buddhism. They normally cannot, as most foreigners find out as they proceed to learn more about Japanese culture.

(3) *Simplification*

The other additional factor which causes problems is the process of *simplification* or *lack of control*. Speech or other behavior may be simplified without either the influence of the native system, or an attempt to approximate the target language. A sentence such as *America kotatsu good?* "Are American *kotatsu* (Japanese foot warmers) good?" simply reduces English grammar to the minimum. Foreign speakers of Japanese often simplify verbal endings and disregard fine lexical differences. As far as communication rules are concerned, Japanese speakers, when using English, tend to simplify topics heavily. Foreign speakers in general often appear as unsophisticated because they cannot raise other than stereotyped basic topics. Another common problem is unexpected laughter; only children, with their still very simple set of communication constraints, laugh whenever something tickles their mind. Furthermore, foreigners often lose control over their hands and legs, and "help themselves" with their hands as they speak. The expression of their emotions often remains uncontrolled and they laugh like children laugh, without any apparent reason.

This simplification of behavior, or lack of control over one's acts, probably affects social and cultural behavior as well, but the question has not been studied as much as linguistic or communicative simplification. One phenomenon which comes immediately to my mind is lavish spending of money by some foreign tourists (which would be carefully checked in native situations). Also, as mentioned above, some foreigners reduce their usual activities to the minimum. People who would definitely go out to play sports and dine out in their native environment, tend to stay in their hotel rooms and eat in the hotel restaurant while overseas.

Of course, not all foreigners in Japan or Japanese overseas are affected. But most people will agree that some of this "simplification" did take place in their own experience. What actually happens here is that we are unable to cope with too many different foreign rules which need to be applied. One returns, in a sense, to the stage when one had not yet acquired all those complicated norms of language, communication, and culture. To a native observer, such foreigners appear like children or unsocialized teenagers.

What follows for "communication learners" is that they cannot simply rely on removing the influence of their native norms. They must also attend to their interim assumptions about language, communication, and culture, and make sure that these approximate more and more the target system. It is also extremely important to realize that the phenomenon of simplification takes place. A simple realization alone will of course not help, but it may be the first step leading to final correction.

Of course, in order to remove problems of communication, measures which are directed at the foreigner do not suffice. We must also give attention to our behavior as native participants. Do we try to understand the problems of those who do not possess the advantage of speaking their own language? Do we try to understand the reasons why problems occur? In a situation of intercultural contact it is easy to suggest that the others should "improve their English." But before they can do that, we are obliged to do as much as we can to make international communication successful.

TWO
RULES OF CULTURE

In the preceding chapter I argued that communication with the Japanese cannot succeed unless we know who the Japanese are. In this chapter I shall attempt to provide a brief outline of some features of Japanese culture and society, knowledge of which is indispensable for foreigners who meet with the Japanese in contact situations.

Let me say here that much miscomprehension already exists and that it affects interpersonal communication and interaction. Few countries and few people have been as unsuccessful as Japan and the Japanese in communicating with the mainstream of the Western world and other nations. Much of this has been the result of the great cultural distance between Japan and the West. However, much also follows from historical configurations and particularly the role of Japan in World War II. Moreover, after World War II, as before, the flow of information has mainly been *to* Japan. Little information came in the opposite direction and the public of other countries had little opportunity to develop and unbiased picture of the present state of Japan's modernization, thought, and life.

It would serve no purpose to glorify Japan. However, any realistic assessment must lead to the conclusion that the perception of contemporary Japan held by foreigners is more often than not outdated, unrealistic, or clearly wrong.

TRADITIONAL AND WESTERN CULTURE IN JAPAN

The Modernization of Japan

One of the basic issues concerns Japan's current position on the path of modernization. Travelers to Japan are often surprised both by the wealth of traditional culture and by the variety of modern cultural forms, and for many it is difficult to sum up: is Japan basically traditional or modern?

A number of stereotyped images persist. Among foreigners living in Japan I met with the conviction that the Japanese split neatly into the traditional and the modern type. The modern, or as it was frequently put, Westernized, Japanese were those who spoke (some) English and actively mixed with foreigners. The traditional Japanese did not. Since I knew some of those who were put in one of the two categories, I could check the validity of the classification. The argument was highly questionable. Those who were labeled "modern/Westernized" spoke perhaps better English but they did not necessarily possess a special amount of knowledge about the West, often did not read much except for Japanese historical romances, and maintained a very traditional relationship with their job superiors. Some of those called "traditional" were just average. But there were others who, their shyness apart, had an unusual understanding of the West gained by extensive reading (in translation), and possessed an utterly modern life style.

In situations of contact the relationship between tradition and Westernization may appear in a distorted fashion. Some basic principles and facts must be understood before we can proceed to a successful relationship with the Japanese.

Modernization and Westernization

In contact with contemporary Japan we must distinguish between the modern and the Western. Modernization is a process through which traditional institutions are replaced by "modern" ones as a consequence of industrialization. For instance, in modern societies families that previously included several generations are usually replaced by "nuclear" families, consisting of parents and dependent children. In modern societies people are more individualistic. Modern culture is characterized by considerable political as well as social freedom and a number of other similar features connected with individualization. On the other hand, Westernization means taking on a particular form of culture, historically derived from the European tradition. For instance, one can speak in Japan of the Westernization of political institutions, of Western music, Western dress, or Western-style housing.

The process of modernization set off in Japan on the basis of internal need for social and cultural change which was brought out by the process of industrialization. There may have been influences from Western societies, but the basic drive was Japanese. Of course, as the process developed, there was a need for more and more modern institutions and things. Since such institutions and things were already available in the West, they were borrowed by the Japanese. For instance, modernization required that a representative political body (such as a diet) be formed. Since such bodies existed in the West, the particulars of the structure and equipment, down to the buckles on the shoes of the doormen, were borrowed from the West. However, the ways in which the resulting institution, the Japanese diet, actually worked were different from the Western ways. One can borrow technology, forms of culture, and individual ideas, but it is much more difficult to imitate the ways in which a society operates. Until after World War II the Japanese diet was an institution of only minor importance in the life of the country and had never played the role it did in the Western democracies. Note that to borrow technology, cultural forms, and ideas during the process of modernization is common to all nations. Of course, European nations were borrowing from each other copiously and mostly without being ashamed at all.

In the case of visitors to Japan, Westernization is of course what attracts much attention. The Western cultural forms are easily identifiable, because they are familiar to the visitor. In the past, amazement and amusement often resulted from the mixture of Japanese and Western forms: a Western hat, a Japanese kimono, and Western galoshes.

Foreigners sometimes express in conversation regret concerning the loss of uniquely Japanese cultural forms and values. On occasions it must be admitted that such criticism is justified. In some cases, however, it does not take into account the necessities of modernization, and this fact may be highly significant for the Japanese we are talking to. Japan could not retain its traditional Buddhist ideologies as the basic component of its modern social thought; the Japanese needed a music which would be more suitable to express the feelings of a modern man than the inherited musical genres, which were loaded with traditional social values and used in traditional contexts; a futon may be esthetically more pleasing than a bed, but many futons may be put in one room, in which only one bed will fit. A bed can thus become a symbol of an individual's strive for privacy and serve as a symbol of modernization.

However, we should realize that among the modern nations of the world Japan has carried over an enormous amount of its traditional culture and values and has successfully integrated them into present-day culture. Hence, contemporary Japan is able to draw on the repertoire of virtually the whole of Western culture as well as the extensive range of purely Japanese cultural forms.

The Present State of the Traditional Culture

Only some of the inherited features of culture are incompatible with modernization. This is true for instance about many features of earlier political structure, family, and ideology. However, many traditional characteristics have nothing to do with the problem of modernization. As long as the overall structure of the daily diet is satisfactory, it doesn't matter whether we eat fish raw or cooked, or drink green or black tea.

Some features of traditional Japanese culture occupy the middle ground between those which have to change with proceeding modernization and those which do not. Many of such features have been temporarily questioned during the process of modernization and some are problematic even today. The famous 17-syllable haiku poems tended to retain their very traditional atmosphere and formal constraints. As Takeo Kuwabara noted early in the postwar period, a modern Japanese justifiably felt that his cultural needs were different. The premodern organization of many traditional arts which lived in closed schools with an *iemoto* (head of the school) on the top could not be easily accepted by modern artists. The traditional narrative arts (*kōdan, naniwa-bushi*, etc.) were found guilty both because of their content and because of their association with the least modernized sector of the society. Many traditional genres exported overseas and greatly admired for their "modern" contribution to world culture correlate, in fact, with a fairly conservative social atmosphere in Japan.

Until relatively recently the traditional style of daily life and participation in traditional cultural genres was characteristic for the lower and upper ends of the social spectrum—the middle classes were carriers of the most strongly "Westernized" lifestyle. People accepted tradition either because they were too poor, or because they were rich enough to afford it. In each case the genres were different. Today, the social distribution of traditional culture seems to be leveling up. Of course, apart from the tradition for the poor and the rich, another distinction was of importance: the traditional culture of the samurai class, and that of the merchant class. For instance, even up until a few decades ago a girl from an originally samurai family, if learning to play a traditional musical instrument, would normally select the *koto* (Japanese harp), while a girl from an originally merchant household would learn the *shamisen* (Japanese guitar). These distinctions, too, seem to be today fatally weakened.

It would be unrealistic to claim that all questions directed to the traditional culture have been answered. Many of the problems still retain their validity. However, since the premodern sector of Japanese economic, political, and social life has now been largely eliminated, the new situation opened the way for incorporating the traditional cultural genres into the overall structure of modern Japanese culture. The internal modernization of the inherited culture will proceed, but the genres will be preserved for the future, not only for Japan but for mankind in general.

Some readers will have the opportunity to meet middle-class Japanese who quite clearly perceive this problematic character of certain components of the traditional cultural genres and assume a critical stance. They are not enthusiastic about Zen Buddhism or haiku and prefer Western philosophy and modern poetry. They do not appreciate classical Japanese music, while being enthusiastic listeners or performers of Bach or Chopin. In general, many of these people are sceptical, perhaps too sceptical, concerning the possible contribution traditional Japanese cultural and social forms could make to world culture.

The "Western" Sector of Japanese Culture

Almost all genres of Western culture, both high-brow and popular, vigorously flourish in Japan. Perhaps this is less surprising for many of us than it was thirty years ago. Any Western literature of any importance has been translated into Japanese and has found avid readers. Some readers prefer Western, some native Japanese (of course, mainly modern) literature, although for some there is no difference. We can assume that an educated Japanese will be familiar with the names and works of major world authors. Of course, one should not expect a taxi driver to be madly in love with Joyce or Kafka. The high-brow culture is still the property of the middle class, in America and Europe, as well as in Japan.

Western classical music could hardly be considered foreign in Japan. It is as much Japanese as it is English, Russian, or Finnish. The Japanese have made a remarkable contribution, if we consider the shortness of time they have participated. A friend who lives in a small overseas country told me the other day with a smile: we are backward, neither the conductor of our symphony orchestra nor the first violin is Japanese. Japanese composition (Mayuzumi, Miyoshi, and others) stands on very firm ground. And Japanese musical education, with the Suzuki or Yamaha method, has certainly made a mark worldwide. It is gratifying to note that some of these contributions to world music are of special interest not merely because they are good music, but because they are both world and Japanese music, drawing in an unobtrusive and sensitive way on the Japanese tradition. Of course, it should be noted that the spread of Western music to virtually all members of the Japanese middle class is a relatively recent phenomenon. For the older generation of Japanese, in particular those who have been brought up in areas other than Tokyo, Western classical music, especially vocal music, is still irrelevant. This fact is of importance when we select topics for conversation in contact situations.

It would be impossible to go through all genres of modern culture in Japan. Let me, however, mention at least another one in which the blending of Western and Japanese elements has been extremely successful. This is Japanese modern architecture, represented by names such as Kenzō Tange, Kishō Kurokawa, or Arata Isozaki. As in music, the important point in this type of architecture is that it does not simply use the exotic and colorful "Japanese" elements. Its success is based on a much more subtle incorporation of the Japanese spirit in its forms. This is what renders it attractive not only for the Japanese but on a worldwide scale.

Foreigners and Traditional Japanese Culture

Many Japanese enjoy providing basic information to foreigners about the traditional sector of Japanese culture. However, this attitude may change if they meet an enthusiastic foreigner who has some previous knowledge and is eager to discuss traditional Japanese culture at length. Foreigners who came to Japan to discuss with the Japanese the excellence of the Kabuki theatre, the beauty of calligraphy, and the wisdom of Zen Buddhism frequently complain that the Japanese do not want to talk to them about these issues.

There are several possible explanations for this behavior. Firstly, it is true that Japanese traditional culture is very complicated and that the average person may not know enough about the subject and will avoid it. Someone who does not compose haiku himself does not know much about the details of the art. What he does know, however, is that there are complicated rules, and he doubts that a foreigner who can hardly communicate in Japanese about matters of daily life can really appreciate them. Although this may not always be a correct assumption, it must be admitted that the understanding of traditional Japanese culture by foreign students or "experts," who claim knowledge in a particular area, does sometimes remain limited and, from the point of view of some Japanese, superficial.

Perhaps more significantly, a number of people in Japan—and many of the Japanese who live overseas—are concerned about the foreigner who is likely to believe that the traditional genres are the only, or perhaps the central, components of contemporary Japanese culture in general. The fact is that Zen, the tea ceremony, *tanka* poetry, or the Bunraku puppet theatre are not the only, or the most important, features of the contemporary cultural scene. To believe that everyone in Japan practices ikebana or that it is a significant

symbol of contemporary Japan is to misunderstand Japan. To see only the traditional sector of Japanese culture and to attribute to it an
exaggerated place within Japanese society, as many foreign en-
thusiasts do, represents a major distortion of a balanced picture of the
country. Some Japanese are afraid of this, and refuse to cooperate.

It is true that Japanese tradition contains values that can greatly
enrich the contemporary culture of other nations. This can certainly
be said about ikebana, Zen, or almost any other component.
However, our own admiration for traditional Japanese culture and
its potential usefulness for the world are one thing; the role of the
traditional elements in contemporary Japan is another. We should
not confuse these two issues. Our interest in Japanese tradition does
not necessarily mean that all Japanese themselves should be looking
at the problem in the same way. Some problems of incomplete
modernization of the social system of Japanese traditional culture,
mentioned above, illustrate the legitimacy of the Japanese stance.
Both points of view are justifiable, but they are different.

JAPAN: ONE OR MANY?

Is There One Single Japan?

When we look at Japan from the outside it appears so different and
exotic. Inevitably we are attracted by the differences and they tend to
cover for us the internal variation within Japanese culture. When
dealing with our own culture we know very well that not everyone
can be expected to be the same. There are usually people of different
regional origin, people of varying social classes, age, and sex,
members of different ethnic groups—say, as in England, the English,
the Scots, the Welsh, Jamaicans, Indians, etc., people who hold
completely different political, social, or cultural views. Even when
we think about citizens of countries that are close to us, such as the
French in the case of England, or the Sri Lankans in the case of India,
we do not assume that they all are the same. An identity of life style,
attitudes, and opinions is never expected.

However, in comparison with the information we possess about
other leading countries of the world, there is still very little informa-

tion available about Japan. There is no systematic teaching about Japan in schools. Apart from South Korea, Australia, and New Zealand the Japanese language is not being widely taught at the secondary level. The mass media everywhere in the world still carries little reliable information. Travel to Japan is limited and necessarily exerts little influence. Moreover, most of the available Western and Japanese sources of information speak about Japan as one undivided body, and individual Japanese informants, too, tend to make statements on behalf of "We Japanese." The situation is highly unsatisfactory and leads to perceptions of Japan that are unrealistic and sometimes biased.

As a consequence of this situation we tend to see Japan as one whole, and the Japanese as all of the same kind. In fact, Japan is as diverse as any other country. To speak of it as of a single and indivisible entity, to say that the Japanese do things this or that way or that they all hold a certain opinion is as unrealistic as to believe that all French were ardent admirers of President Pompidou. Foreigners would indeed have little chance to understand the Japanese and communicate with them if they did not understand what kind of Japanese they are communicating with.

Regional Differences

One of the differences which normally remains hidden for foreign visitors is the difference of regional background. Of course, there is the urban-rural distinction which remains alive, even if people in the rural sectors are well off and supplied with modern machinery and appliances to the same extent as the urban Japanese. However, few Japanese of rural origin usually appear in contact situations, unless we live or undertake extensive travel in the rural areas.

Although dwarfed by comparison with the huge neighboring continent, Japan is indeed a large country and internal divisions have naturally developed in the course of her long history. For instance, the Japanese sometimes feel quite strongly about the difference between the Kantō and the Kansai regions. Kantō is the area around Tokyo; Kansai covers Kyoto, Osaka, and the environs. Though both clearly Japanese, the cultural traditions of these two areas are quite different. The language sounds different, the food tastes different, and there are different traditions in art and daily life. The Kansai tradition is based on the long history of Japan before the modern period, when Kyoto was the main political and cultural centre of Japan, and on the traditional economic strength of Osaka. Of course, Osaka and Kyoto are still an extremely important part of Japan, but it is a fact that the political center of the country moved to Tokyo as early as the seventeenth century, that even the emperor moved in 1868, and that, hesitantly, the head offices of the biggest corporations followed the general trend after World War II, if not earlier.

On the other end of the scale we find those regions which, for a number of reasons, only developed their modern eocnomy and culture relatively recently. Because of this, people from these regions have always been the object of discrimination. For long, the Tōhoku region, located immediately to the northeast of Tokyo, has been the source of cheap labor for the capital. Another such area is the Ryūkyū islands, whose dialects, although clearly Japanese, are totally incomprehensible to speakers of any other variety of Japanese; at the end of World War II they suffered enormous losses and some of them (Okinawa) were later under direct US rule.

Another important difference is that between those parts of Japan which face the Pacific (*Omote Nihon* "the outward Japan") and those which adjoin the Japan Sea (*Ura Nihon* "the outback Japan"). The latter, apart from specific trends in traditional rural social structure, is known for its harsh climatic conditions, so different from what foreigners usually imagine or know as Japan.

Regional identity is strong among the Japanese, and, even when resident overseas, people tend to meet more often when they possess the same regional background. Kantō, particularly Tokyo Japanese, are currently those who have an advantage. Others are expected to adapt their behavior and give up their regional characteristics. A strong opposition is sometimes felt against this trend, in particular by people from the Kansai area.

Class Distinctions

Distinctions in social class are also among those that are likely to escape the attention of foreign visitors. The matter obviously is not that foreigners should learn to underestimate some Japanese on the basis of their social class. It is true that too much attention paid to the social origin of one's interlocutors may be harmful. However, distinctions do exist, and it is useful to be familiar with them. Many handbooks compiled for foreigners claim on an optimistic note that "there are relatively few class and status distinctions in Japanese society." However, this statement is obviously untrue.

It must be admitted that for an average citizen the premodern and prewar nobility have ceased existing as political, economic, or cultural entities. However, centuries of privileged treatment for the nobility, the former samurai class, and the old rich families, are still instrumental in placing their descendents in advantaged situations within the education system and result in their domination of the leading positions within the society. To readers from countries with a past dominated by aristocracy, this situation will not appear as specific to Japan.

In surveys of public opinion, approximately ninety percent of the Japanese consistently describe themselves as "middle class." This descriptor signifies for them little, and the fact should not be taken very seriously. Although access to education, including higher education, is in Japan available quite freely, it is of course children from families which already do possess education who have a distinct advantage. In this respect, again, Japan is no different from any other modern society. Since positions which lead to the upper middle class status normally require graduation from a very good university, they are not easily accessible to everyone. Neither is mixing of people from the middle class and the working class through marriage more simple than in other advanced societies. Class barriers which may not be quite obvious to a foreigner may be significant and strong for the Japanese.

However, one frequent misunderstanding should be dispelled. While in some societies the less wealthy classes may be described as uneducated, this is not, in general, true about Japan. General education has been widely accessible in Japan, and most workers will be high school graudates, especially if they are relatively young.

The majority of the Japanese which a foreigner, unless he is a resident in Japan, is likely to meet in contact situations are middle-class people mostly from Tokyo. So are the authors of most books and articles about Japan we are likely to read, and we should realize that our perception of Japan will tend to be most strongly influenced by this unrepresentative sample of the population of Japan. Foreigners should certainly try to break this spell of circumstances and attempt to meet as many other Japanese as they can.

Sex and Age

As in most other modern societies, differences in sex and age are significant. In the case of Japan, women communicate politeness more strongly than men. They always seem to behave in a deferential way, give precedence to men, bow lower, and even help men into their coats. These forms of etiquette do of course reflect the subordinate position of women, but the degree of subordination may not always be as strong as would appear to Western observers who interpret the behavior through their own behavioral norms. It is true that women are not normally represented on the upper levels of decision making in the society, are underestimated, and in employment underpaid. Again, this all is not unfamiliar in any modern society. However, the women's liberation movement, the movement for the removal of sexist discrimination in language, and other similar movements are neither as extensive nor as radical as in other developed nations.

Yet, it would be a mistake to assume that Japanese women are toys in the hands of men, totally subjugated to them. Though not equal, in many areas of social and economic life women play an important role; as I shall explain later, they certainly have a strong say in most family matters.

In some Asian societies, age is a very important component of status. This is not in general true of Japan. Although many leading politicians and captains of the economy are very old, old age alone does not automatically guarantee the right to esteem.

The most common retirement age in Japan is 60. Although for some this means that they can commence their "second life," and although highly situated officials or executives are welcome in various organizations or smaller companies (where the retirement age is higher), for many retirement brings a considerable decrease in their income and is not something people look forward to.

Dual Structure of the Japanese Economy

When foreigners deal with people employed in the Japanese system, they frequently do not realize the importance of variation between the size of enterprizes and working conditions. It has often been asserted that Japanese organizations are characterized by features such as life-long employment, seniority wage system, and a number of fringe benefits available to the employees. However, it has mostly remained unsaid that these conditions only exist in the large companies, which employ not more than twenty percent of the Japanese workforce at the most. There is usually a radical difference between these large companies (*daikigyō*) and medium-or-small companies (*chūshō kigyō*) which struggle for survival whenever the Japanese economy shows a downward trend. Of course, there is a considerable difference in wages in the two groups. Since the large leading companies were accepting employees immediately upon graduation, one's future was decided when one finished school. Until very recently, it was virtually impossible to obtain a position in a large company except at the beginning of one's career.

Company executives in Western capitalist countries show high professional mobility. For a Japanese company man (*sararīman*) it is much more difficult to change his employer, in particular if he belongs to one of the large enterprises. A decision to leave and settle down overseas needs much more courage than in the case of an American or an Australian. The possibility that he might return to a Japanese employer under comparable conditions is at present still very small.

Ethnic Composition

The Japanese themselves quite often assert that the country is ethnically totally homogeneous. They may have a case in comparison with countries in which fifty percent or more of the population is of varying ethnical background. However, Japan, too has its minorities, and they are not of a negligible size.

The undisputably largest minority are the Koreans, who were brought to Japan, sometimes as forced cheap labor, during the years of Japan's occupation of Korea (1910-45). The total number still exceeds 600,000. They have always been the object of discrimination. Some of them have assimilated, but most others, even if they may have lost their original language, wish to maintain their Korean identity. In comparison, the Chinese minority is smaller (approximately 40,000 people) and consists of several groups which partly retain their original Chinese dialects. The number of foreigners, those who are not permanent residents living in Japan, is growing and will certainly further increase in the future. At the end of 1986 the number was 867,237 including permanent residents. This figure did not include American military personnel in Japan.

An important, though small minority, is that of the Ainu, who originally inhabited most of the Japanese archipelago, but have now been restricted to the northern island of Hokkaido. Owing to a former policy of eradication and the lack of official support, the Ainu language (which is totally different from Japanese) is almost extinct. However, over 20,000 people are still registered as of Ainu origin. The feeling of an ethnic identity is growing.

In agreement with the theory of a monoethnic Japan, the Japanese government has never provided any support for the minorites. For the politican and the bureaucracy the issue does not exist.

A special problem often completely hidden to casual observers, is the existence of a sizeable community of untouchables, the *burakumin*. Although ethnically Japanese, they have been strongly discriminated against. The attribution to them of a separate identity was based on the fact that they engaged in occupations which were traditionally considered as "unclean" (such as killing animals, or using animal skin, for instance, in making footwear). The *burakumin* are particularly numerous in some areas of the Kansai region.

The Government and the People

The theory of *Japan Incorporated* has depicted the country as consiting of one brain and one body. The theory suggests that the whole nation moves in concert, under the leadership of the government, toward achieving a common aim: the maximum profit for Japan. Although there are certainly consultations between the government and private bodies, the theory is false. It relies too heavily on the wrong perception of Japan as a monolithic whole.

We frequently meet with statements which refer to the acts of the Japanese government and suggest that "the Japanese" hold this or that opinion, or have behaved or will behave in a particular way. In the case of France or Germany, it would hardly occur to us that the population would simply and unconditionally identify with the pronouncements and deeds of the government of the day. However, in the case of Japan, with regard to which still a very small amount of information circulates in the international networks, some people easily accept this assumption.

The Japanese government has been in the hands of a single party, the Liberal Democratic Party, since the end of World War II (except for a very short period of time in 1949), but this does not imply that there is no effective alternative to the government's views and policies in Japan. The fact that the Liberal Democrats have been systematically returned to power indicates that the party has strong support among the voters. However, it is necessary to realize that the popular vote for the party does not substantially exceed fifty percent. The support for the government has been strong among the rural population and weaker in the cities. Much of the country's intellectual élite has always been critical, or at least uncommitted.

Although some factions and policies of the Liberal Democratic Party are reminiscent of prewar Japan, to assume that the government on the whole is ultrarightist would be grave mistake. It would be equally misleading to believe that the opposition is a bunch of irresponsible radicals. The largest opposition party is that of the Socialists; following it are the Komeito (Clean Government Party), the Democratic Socialists, and the Communist Party of Japan, which attracts a relatively large vote (approximately ten percent). There are also some smaller parties represented in the Japanese Diet.

The voice of the opposition is much more clearly heard in Japan than overseas. Since none of the opposition parties has shown much interest in the image of Japan overseas, the government, through its Foreign Ministry and diplomatic missions, has remained virtually the only spokesman for Japan abroad. This is of course a common practice of most countries of the world. However, in view of the scarcity of information available about Japan, as compared with information about other leading countries of the world, the image of Japan as guided by a single political and social platform still survives.

HOW DO THEY THINK?

To know what people think about their own society and the world is of primary importance when we communicate with them. Yet, with regard to Japan, this is one of the most neglected areas. Books about Japan usually deal with its history and economic achievements, or describe places or daily life. When they make a detour into the area of thought, they often deal with Zen philosophy, Buddhism, the prewar nationalistic theories, or try to make very wide and stereotypic generalizations about the "Japanese mind," usually based on little evidence. For an average visitor, the ways of thought and attitudes to the world and life of a contemporary Japanese mostly remain hidden behind the barrier of language and non-verbal behavior. Some members of the foreign community in Japan may live in the country for years without gaining much insight into what the people they are meeting daily actually think. The area is vast and the following comments may only deal briefly with some of the most important issues.

Present-day Nationalism

Are the Japanese nationalists? As with most questions that use the unqualified category "Japan" or "the Japanese," there is no simple answer. The feeling that Japan is very special and is, or should be, the best, depends on age, education, urbanization, and political or social conservatism. There was much less variation before World War II when most Japanese were strongly nationalistic, and some people in the West are now afraid that the country might be moving in the same direction again.

However, not even during the war did all young men fulfill the expectations of the nationalistic ideologists of the government. When dying on the battlefield they were supposed to shout "*Tennō heika, banzai* "Long live the Emperor!," but it is well known that many cried out *Okāsan* "Mother!" instead. As a matter of fact, the occupation authorities in postwar Japan were surprised to find how insignificant was the militant ultra-nationalistic opposition to the occupation which they expected.

The immediate postwar generation, especially college graduates who completed their education in the second half of the 1940s or in the 1950s, probably belong to the group of people who are least happy with Japan, and who are prone to believe that anything Western is superior to anything Japanese.

The younger generation—and there seems to be little variation here—grew up in a period which revived the sense of national achievement. Although active nationalism is restricted to an extremely small number of ultra-right-wingers, the young people do accept that there is much Japan can be proud of. By the way, they are right. However, my impression is that in contact situations even the young people will not be unreasonably sensitive and will be prepared to accept a convincing argument.

It should be noted that the politically conservative try to reinforce the "patriotism" of the young generation. Over the last decades some national symbols, out of popularity since the war, have been the object of open political controversies and have been strongly pushed back for official recognition. This concerns the national flag and anthem, official worship at Yasukuni Shrine in Tokyo (where those who died "for the Emperor" or "for their country," including both the Pacific War casualties and those condemned as criminals by the military tribunal of the US occupation forces, are enshrined), and the content of school textbooks, which has been guided by the Education Ministry toward a more positive evaluation of the past. Although supported by the Old Right, these trends should not necessarily be taken for proof that Japan is simply returning to its prewar nationalistic stance. There is little to indicate that nationalism would be taking over the minds of all Japanese and dominate them, as it did before World War II.

There are various popular theories proposing that Japanese culture is completely unique. They are not, however, normally connected with the old-fashioned, prewar style of nationalism; neither do all of them propound that anything Japanese is perfect; neither do they represent the dominant stream of Japanese social science. If anything, the average Japanese—under the influence of the country's slow progress toward internationalization—is moving further and further away from what we would call nationalism.

There is no need to say that the Japanese are likely to support their own team in international sports competitions. But aren't attitudes like that common everywhere in the world? They do not necessarily signify that the old Japanese nationalism "is coming back."

The Emperor

The highest national symbol of prewar Japan was the emperor. It will not be necessary to say that attitudes toward the emperor and the imperial family have vastly changed since World War II. The emperor is not a god any more. There is no need for us to be unduly careful when the issue becomes the topic of discussion in a contact situation. Many intellectuals are simply unconcerned. However, public opinion surveys show that he is not unpopular, and there is a section of the population, often genuine and well meaning, who hold very warm feelings with regard to the imperial family. Some social critics point to the fact that the institution could be used, in the future, to support conservative trends in the society. This indeed might happen but the odds are against a nationalistic upsurge at the moment.

Japan, Militarism, and War

No doubt, the prestige of the army and the navy in prewar Japan was very high. However, things have changed. The Japanese constitution forbids Japan to declare war and to keep a regular army, and although Japan does have a very sizeable military establishment, it cannot use descriptors such as ''the army'' or ''the navy'' and thus refers to itself as the ''Self-Defense Force.'' Its influence within the society is meager. Japan is currently using only about one percent of its national income on the Self-Defense Force, although there are elements within the conservative camp which would like to use more.

Somehow the world failed to register the lesson the Japanese have taken from World War II and from Hiroshima and Nagasaki. In the postwar period the vast majority of the population have grown highly critical of the role of Japan in the war and have become most genuinely committed to the idea of world peace and the removal of the nuclear threat. Most families still retain memories of their relatives who died in China, in the Philippines, or during the air raids, or who starved to death in the immediate postwar period. Annual observances are held at Hiroshima and Nagasaki and are well noted by the nation and the world.

It will not be necessary in contact situations to convince an average Japanese of the significance of the nuclear threat and the necessity to further the cause of world peace. On the contrary, it may be the Japanese who are the more concerned party.

Of course, some of those who were responsible for the wartime situations are still alive and hold important positions in the society. The conservative forces, which are not negligible, try to draw a more acceptable picture of the war and persuade members of the old generation, who have sentimental ties with prewar Japan, and the young generation, who lack immediate experience, that not everything was black. Whatever the results of this reappraisal of the war may be, it is most unlikely that they could affect the majority of the population. In any case, there is no reason to believe that Japan would in the foreseeable future embark on any new military adventure. The old Japanese militarism is dead.

What will be the details of future development depends not merely on the position of the Japanese and the US government but also on the growth and transformations of Japanese peace and anti-nuclear movement. Although the movement attracts strong popular support, its leadership has so far been in the hands of professional politicians and its effectiveness has been marred by factional fights.

Social and Political Thought

Much misunderstanding exists with regard to what the Japanese think about their own society and its organization. Understandably, it would again be difficult to ignore variation in this respect. In general we can say that those who are content with the way society operates will emphasize existing and traditional values while people who do not prefer the current state of affairs naturally maintain a more pessimistic assessment.

The former category of people may present the foreigner with a view of Japan that does not place much stress on variation in society and highlights harmony rather than conflict. The theory that Japanese society is strongly harmonious, that both management and employees cheerfully work toward a common aim, has strong support in Japan. Within this strata of the Japanese there is relatively little interest in social issues, except for those who are engaged professionally in studying or managing social or political affairs. People in postwar Japan used to be very strongly interested in social problems, but since the period of high economic growth (the 1960s) the younger generation, in particular, has grown cooler and shows little social awareness.

On the other hand, those socially and politically less satisfied tend to make a more critical assessment. Many of them will draw on the basically Marxist thinking about society which was extremely strong in the postwar period, even though it receded during the high-economic growth period of the 1960s and 1970s. These people are likely to point to the remnants of premodern elements in Japanese society and the ways they operate on the political level. They will argue that the harmony that is said to exist in Japan only exists on the surface and will point to the considerable number of anti-establishment movements in the society.

Social and political radicalism does exist, and extends both to the right and to the left of the sociopolitical spectrum. Visitors to Japan will notice in particular ultra-rightist nationalists who campaign with great vigor in the streets against virtually everyone, with unofficial blessing from the conservative sections of the establishment. The ultra-left extremists are well known from the periods of the active student movements, and owing to their participation in international terrorist organizations. The average citizen will know that their current strength and support is negligible. Those socially more involved may also express concern with regard to the way these extremist currents connect with other less extreme trends existing within the society.

Movements directed against various forms of discrimination, so popular in other developed countries of the world, frequently receive the support of the media, but in general lag behind the expected level. Sex discrimination often remains unnoticed or unopposed. The idea of discrimination on the basis of age is very unusual. Environmental pollution is opposed with hesitation and little vigor. As mentioned above, the antiwar and anti-nuclear movement command high prestige but do not yet present an effective challenge to the established political institutions.

Are the Japanese Religious?

One of the questions of considerable importance for everybody who is meeting the Japanese, is whether, to what extent, and in what ways they are religious. Many foreigners expect that a society with an Asian background would as a matter of course be strongly committed to religious beliefs. Some expect that the Japanese are all Shintoists, others that they are all Buddhists. Few facts are known.

Official statistics of members of various Japanese religions list about 220 million believers. This is almost twice the entire population of Japan and the statistics alone signal that the problem of Japanese religiosity is not simple.

The original Japanese religion was Shinto, but relatively little of the original Shinto has remained. In the Meiji era some elements of the religion were systematized and transformed into the official religious ideology of the State. Today, although shrines exist, festivals and observances are held, and many beliefs survive in folk customs, Shinto is virtually dead as an organized religion. There are no believers in the proper sense of the word. Wedding ceremonies, sometimes the presentation of a child at the local shrine, and festivals are the only occasions on which a little bit of a religious significance remains. However, one should consider that Christian weddings are also popular in contemporary Japan, without this necessarily meaning, for the people concerned, any deep involvement in Christianity.

Secondly, in the majority of the traditional sects Buddhist priests have turned into religiously passive guardians of the tradition and performers of funeral ceremonies. Still, while virtually no contemporary Japanese will claim that they are Shintoists, one can meet many people who claim that they are Buddhist. Mostly this claim is based on the registration of the family with a particular Buddhist temple which is performing the family's funeral ceremonies. The head of a household keeps tablets with the names of deceased members of the household in a special home "altar" (*butsudan*), and the altar becomes the central point for remembering such members through offerings and prayers. Such acts are based on the feeling of love and indebtedness to the deceased members of one's family, and to speak of them as a manifestation of a religious "cult of ancestors" would be a very far-reaching interpretation. However, except for some, mostly people from the rural areas, there is no other participation. For urban Japanese, Buddhist observances other than the funeral and subsequent memorial ceremonies hardly exit. They normally have only a vague idea about the Buddhist teachings, to say nothing about the difference between one's own sect and other sects of Buddhism.

Some families also keep a Shinto "altar" (*kamidana*), where paper strips obtained at a shrine may be kept for good luck. Annual Shinto shrine festivals play an important role for many people in traditional rural and urban communities. A number of folk religion traits persist in the country, even if in many cases it may be difficult to distinguish between what is a folk custom, a superstition, and a religious belief.

Shinto shrines count people who live in their areas, and Buddhist temples those who use their funeral services as "believers." This accounts for the seemingly illogical statistics quoted above.

It should be noted that Buddhism and Shinto have never been kept strictly apart. These two religions, as well as religious elements from other systems (Confucianism, Taoism, and Christianity) have always been freely utilized by the same people according to the requirements of the situation.

It is still relatively little known that along with Shintoism and Buddhism, a number of "New Religions" has developed on the basis of either the traditional Shinto doctrines (e.g., the Tenri Religion) or Buddhist teachings (e.g., the Soka Gakkai). They are real religions with the active participation of the believers and with specific doctrines. Most of them initially developed as religions for the poor and as such commanded little respect, although the situation is now changing in the case of some of them. The Soka Gakkai, for instance, has a membership of almost 8 million households, and is closely associated with the Komeito, one of the most influential opposition political parties in Japan. Quite a few of these new religions are also active overseas, drawing support among the local Japanese communities, and, to a lesser extent, among completely non-Japanese populations.

The number of Christians in Japan is low. However, it is not unusual to met a Japanese who is either a formal or practicing Christian. The distinctions between various Christian religions are not as pronounced for the Japanese as for many Westerners. This sometimes causes a surprise.

In conversation religion is not taboo. Modern university-educated Japanese, even if not actively belonging to any existing organized religion, are not anti-religious. They see the advantages of a religion and some regret that they have not received more information about religion in their childhood.

Even if not active members of a church, most people share some basic religious attitudes, many of which derive from the original Shinto. These include a concern for purity and thankfulness to the previous generations of one's family. In shrines, temples, and churches people can "pray," thanking god and asking for help. However, a regular participation in observances and the knowledge of organized doctrines are limited to a relatively small number of members of the old religions, and to members of the new religions. In the case of ninety-nine percent of those Japanese with whom foreigners are likely to be in contact, a strong religious attitude cannot be expected to appear.

What Do They Think about Us?

Many foreigners ask what the Japanese actually think about them and about their countries. It has been pointed out by many sociologists that people in Japan distinguish clearly between Caucasians and foreigners from Asia and Africa. While the former enjoy a high status, the latter are not always welcome to the same extent. Some Asian students in Japan complain that they are mistaken for local Koreans and treated in an unfriendly way. This discrimination is not usually strong or overt, and is not a general phenomenon. Even visitors from Asia carry one feature which makes them sought after and appreciated: their command of English is usually much superior to that of their Japanese contacts. However, discrimination is a traditional feature of Japanese life and is not likely to completely disappear overnight. The same is, of course, true about many contemporary Western nations, even though the attitudes to race have started changing in a radical way in the 1960s. Let me add that during the American occupation of Japan, many Japanese willingly joined in distinguishing between the white and black soldiers and discriminating against the latter.

Since the Meiji era, the Japanese have always looked toward Europe and America as the places from which they could learn. The process went so far that much of Western culture was incorporated into Japanese culture in a way that makes it difficult to separate. In the past centuries Japan was always learning from China; in the period of modernization a distinct and conscious trend appeared that forced Japan to turn away from Asia and move closer to the West. Only recently has Asia been receiving more attention again. In particular, public interest in China is overwhelming. Yet, the majority of the average Japanese still feel that their own idenity lies closer to Europe and America than to Asia.

Many foreigners who live in Japan live very happily. Some, however, complain of only being accepted in their role as foreigners, and being rejected if they attempt to speak Japanese or enter existing Japanese networks as equals. Of course, foreigners have a practical value. As mentioned above, they are the source of English in a society in which access to practicing the language is extremely rare. However, those foreigners who are prepared to give as well as to take, and who are prepared to yield—for instance, to accept that the right etiquette norms are not necessarily their own, or to invest some effort into improving their Japanese pronounication—will probably find that they will be accepted reasonably well. Of course, the acceptance by an established network can be difficult in Japan not merely for a foreigner. The Japanese also find it difficult and there is no reason why foreigners should expect to have an immediate free access to any network they fancy to enter. The number of people in Japan who are used to working with foreigners is increasing and they accept foreigners as equal partners in their networks. What perhaps could have been a kind of discrimination before is quickly disappearing.

Education

Since the ways people think are to a large extent influenced by their education, let me add a few words about this aspect of Japanese social life.

In Japan school starts at the age of seven and after six years of primary education, children must complete another three years of a "middle school" to finalize their compulsory education. However, very few students leave school at that stage. More than ninety percent of them continue to the (senior) high school level, from which thirty-five percent proceed to higher education.

At the higher level there are universities or colleges (*daigaku*, four years) as well as junior colleges (*tanki daigaku*, two years). The number of institutions of higher education is enormous. There are more than 200 in Tokyo alone, some of them big, but most rather small. Since considerable differences exist in the assumed or real quality of their programs, to say that someone graduated from "the university in Tokyo" makes very little sense. The University of Tokyo (with capital U, in Japanese often abbreviated as *Tōdai*) and the Kyoto University and Osaka University for the Kansai area are on the top of the hierarchy. At the next level there are a number of public and some private universities (such as Keiō or Waseda). A number of the smaller universities specialize in one or several areas and they may be very good in those disciplines; so it is not easy to make an overall judgment about educational and academic levels.

To know from what university your partner graduated means to know a lot about him or her. Japan hands usually acquire through accumulated experience a list of universities and their ratings. It is important to remember who went where, because people who are graduates of the same university often have a feeling of being close to each other. Common acquaintances, either former students or teachers, are discussed. Yet, one sometimes hesitates to ask directly; the person concerned may have attended a third-rate institution, which does not reflect his current position or aspirations.

From a very early stage Japanese education is geared toward examinations. Even to be accepted to some of the good kindergartens, children have to pass an examination. Places at public and good private junior and senior high schools are scarce, and again, an examination must be passed. The most difficult of all examinations is the university entrance examination, on which much of an individual's future depends: remember that most employers accept job applicants according to which university their degree is from. The examination system makes life hell for many Japanese children and represents one of the most serious setbacks of the Japanese education system. Competition for places at the most prestigeous institutions is fierce, and much depends not so much on the candidate's actual knowledge as on the art of sitting for an examination. However, once admitted to the university, everyone will pass.

Many manuals on Japanese education state that after World War II the education system has been Americanized. Indeed, the number of years one spends in the primary school, the middle (junior high) school, the (senior) high school, and at the university are the same. Also, the university (college) system, is based on the same principle of general edcuation, followed by programs composed of a large number of relatively freely selected small "units." However, even if the form is similar, the content of work differs a great deal. The orientation toward examinations has already been mentioned. There is also emphasis on rote learning. At all levels of education it is the teacher who speaks; the students remain passive recipients of knowledge. At the college (university) level, in particular in the humanities and social science disciplines, students simply take notes at lectures and pass examinations on the basis of memorizing their teacher's talks. The number of classes called *zemi* (seminar), at which the students can discuss some problems related to their discipline, is very limited. Teachers, who normally are present at the university only for their classes, are not bound to follow any approved curricula. The course develops as it proceeds, and normally finishes at a much lower stage than both the teacher and the students had expected.

This dim picture of Japanese education, common among foreign observers, may actually be culturally biased. For instance, one can argue that Japanese children receive a much more systematic summary of knowledge about the world than most of their Western counterparts, that the ability to think in a clear way is not so much bound to discussions in the classroom, and that the loose character of the college (university) curricula provide the students with the opportunity to read much more widely about man and society according to their own selection. In any case, the outcomes of the education system are not bad. Japan certainly has produced many excellent specialists and academics, as well as top company executives and administrators. The question is whether it could do better if the content of its educational system were also "Westernized."

FAMILY AND FRIENDSHIP

The Japanese Family

One of the typical complaints of short-term visitors to Japan is that there is no opportunity to visit a sufficient number of Japanese families to form an opinion on how the Japanese behave within their natural family network. To be invited to visit a Japanese home has recently become easier, but owing to housing problems and the lack of confidence of many people who fear that they cannot successfully entertain a foreigner at home, not all visitors to Japan have had the experience. What the structure and daily life of a Japanese family is still remains for many an unanswered question.

In the 1980s approximately eighty percent of all Japanese households consisted of an elementary (nuclear) family or of single unmarried persons. A nuclear family includes husband and wife, or a single parent, and unmarried children. In the first half of the 1980s a typical Japanese family had one or two children, rarely more. The time of families with a large number of children is necessarily gone and even if the average may slightly increase, it does not seem that the pattern would change to any significant extent.

Typical Misunderstandings

A number of misunderstandings about the Japanese family has been perpetuated in the West. One of them concerns its composition. On the analogy of some Asian countries foreigners often expect the Japanese family to be a large complicated structure, including several generations and within each generation a number of families. However, the fact is that this pattern was abandoned in Japan relatively early in its post-medieval history. Even though various ties between people of the same parentage continued to be acknowledged, the successor (and his successors)—usually the eldest son—was the only one to live with his parents after marriage, while other sons and daughters moved out of the parental home when they married and created separate families.

The pattern of the parents and the eldest son living together appears today in approximately fifteen percent of households. The percentage is lower in the urban areas and higher in the country, where the family occupation (farmer, traditional artisan, or craftsman) requires more hands as well as continuity of experience. The pattern also provides a sort of old-age social security. However, even where parents live with their children, the relationship is changing and does not involve domination by the older generation. This is particularly true in the cities, where the living together of two adult generations, even if also emotionally gratifying, is primarily a matter of convenience resulting from housing shortage, the need for baby sitters, and the unsatisfactory level of old-age pensions. Often, the child with whom the parents live is not the eldest son, as in the traditional system, but any child who possesses the necessary facilities.

Another frequent misinterpretation is the belief that the Japanese family is a tight hierarchical structure in which the husband (often absent for most of the day and evening) is a tyrannical despot of whom all the others are afraid. First, the absence of the husband is a point which is often exaggerated. He may be frequently late, and, if he is an executive in a large company, may be entertaining company guests several times a week. Men who are not company executives may be absent occasionally, but not daily throughout the year. If they are away, they often work overtime to speed up the repayment of a housing loan or to cover educational expenses. The reasons for their absence are appreciated by their families. Of course, there are increasingly more and more cases of husbands transferred by their employers to a different city, who live separately from their families and only "commute" home. All these cases constitute real social problems, but they should not be taken to mean that no men in Japan are present at home any time, as the case is often presented. It must also be added that the husband and father is not a tyrant. As everywhere, there are men with despotic inclinations, but most Japanese men are as kind and considerate as men in any other society.

Roles of Family Members

In theory, roles within a Japanese family are relatively clearly defined. The husband works outside, while his wife remains at home, looking after the house and the children. The image is not so different from that of a Western family some thirty years ago. Like in the West, this is only an ideal: in present-day Japan more than fifty percent of all women are employed, and that of course includes many married women with children. Like in the West not so many years ago, almost all household work is carried out by the wife. However, unlike in the West, the authority of the wife is strong within her own domain. Foreigners are often surprised to hear that family budgets are controlled in Japan by wives, and that husbands are only given a daily allowance for their personal expenses! This is not an exception but the rule. Many decisions in the family domain can be taken by the wife alone, even if on important issues the husband is of course consulted.

The behavior of little children is not strongly regulated. Pressure to conform with social norms is usually exerted relatively late, and with Japanese families that live overseas this sometimes causes problems, especially if there are visitors to the family. The range of behavior in which such pre-school children are allowed to engage at home or in public, inclusive of physical aggression against parents, is much wider than what middle-class families would tolerate in most Western countries. On the other hand, school age children are usually very well disciplined. They spend less time than Western children in playing in general, and study more, preparing for the next entrance examinations. A much less intensive pattern of many overseas schools often causes problems of adjustment for Japanese children who attend school overseas and subsequently return to live in Japan.

Neither the father nor the mother normally make decisions concening the marriage of their children. The percentage of arranged marriages (*miai*) has dropped to under thirty percent, but even when the first meeting is arranged, the young people can normally decide on thier own whether the relationship will be further developed or finish with the first encounter. Since thought had been given by other people to the choice of the partner, arranged marriages are usually successful and often lead to an increasingly affectionate relationship between the husband and the wife. Still, most young people express a preference for a ''love marriage'' and some of those whose marriages were arranged prefer not to eloborate on the topic.

Modernization of the Japanese Family

Quite a few foreign observers speak about the ''Western influence'' on the Japanese family, as if an institution as basic as the family could be changed under the influence of imported ideas. In fact, the recent changes in the Japanese family are not the result of ''Westernization'' but of an internal process of ''modernization'' of the society. It is industrialization that has led to the situation in which the younger generation moves to the city, leaving the older people behind, or in which it more recently moves from one city to another, breaking the traditional ties; industrialization has resulted in the radical decrease in the number of farming households and renders the extensive family structure unnecessary; the independence of the nuclear family has been reinforced by the indepedent position of each individual in employment.

The traditional family undoubtedly had its weaknesses. However, so does the "modern" one. While the traditional family was a very stable unit, the modern Japanese family offers a much looser environment. One side-effect of this situation is that in present-day Japan divorce has already reached the same level as in France or West Germany. Children are the ones who suffer most from the loss of the firm and protective structure of the old family and the disorientation of the transitional period. Recent problems with child violence in classrooms and against weaker classmates indicates the scope of the problems.

Another problem that Japanese families face results from the fact that Japan has the highest life expectancy in the world. The percentage of old people in the population is growing fast and the percentage of the very old, who cannot look after themselves, is increasing still faster. This fact not merely threatens to ruin Japan's superannuation funds but also poses the question of whether the percentage of those who live with their aged parents will further decrease or start increasing again. These issues are very much discussed in Japan and it is not unlikely that they will appear as a topic in contact situations.

Friendship

Interaction with Japan would have little lasting sense if we did not include as one of our major aims the establishment of friendship with the Japanese. Yet sociologists and anthropologists are still unable to provide any reliable guidance in this area. How is friendship normally established in Japan? Can it be established and maintained in situations of contact between the Japanese and foreigners? Foreign visitors and residents in Japan sometimes complain about the lack of friends. Others have many friends and are prepared to declare that the institution of friendship is nowhere as enjoyable or rewarding as in Japan. What are the facts, and what should we do?

People from socially very advanced industrial societies such as the USA, Canada, or Australia, where relations between people tend to become informal faster than anywhere else, should not identify the category of friendship in Japan with that of their own culture. In Japan the concept of "a friend" covers a wide range of relationships between two extreme points: one is a simple *tomodachi* (friend); the second is referred to as *shin'yū* (close friend). (Of course, in everyday conversation the less assuming word *tomodachi* "friend" is often used to account for both). Both of the two forms of friendship are less casual than what we are likely to call "being a friend" in America or in Australia. Meeting someone at a party or having had a meal together may entitle us in our own culture to the use of first names and to a somewhat casual attitude. In Japan, more contact is necessary to reach even the first point of the scale of friendship. The last stage of the relationship can only be entered on the basis of a long and well-established contact, such as occurs when people grow up together, or work together for some period of time. The latter type of friendship is usually limited to those who are approximately of the same age. People of very different age or social status can be friends in our sense of the word, but do not usually qualify for all the privileges of even the first stage of the *tomodachi* relationship. The relationship in this case will normally be somewhat different, with one of the two being a senior, the other a junior. The situation resembles the situation in Europe a few decades ago.

All this does not imply that the Japanese are formal all the time, do not chat, joke, or in general relax when communicating with casual acquaintances. However, it seems to be true that the informal style of interaction is assumed after a somewhat longer period of time.

Friendship and Foreigners

What I have said so far does not, of course, automatically apply in situations of contact between the Japanese and foreigners. Occasionally you may meet people who feel that it is difficult to establish a friendship with a foreigner. However, such people will be rare. More often concessions are made. The time necessary for the commencement of an informal relationship may be shortened, the age may become irrelevant. Foreigners who meet the Japanese should carefully watch how the relationship is developing and if they can see signs of uneasiness in the case of their Japanese contact, should better refrain from pushing for an early informal tie. Of course, the matter is delicate, because if their reticence is interpreted as an indication that informality is undesirable, the fact may have a decisive effect on the developing relationship.

In a relationship between two Japanese the first stage of friendship does include rights to informal communication, though hardly ever the right to call someone by first name, or to completely reduce the usual range of honorifics. In contact situations much will depend on the previous experience of the Japanese participants. Some of those who possess a long experience of meeting foreigners do not mind using first names at all. Others may hesitate. It should be remembered that even when first names are not used, the closeness of the relationship may be considerable.

Friendship brings duties as well as privileges. As a general statement, necessarily simplifying the complex issue, we could perhaps say that the most important duty of a simple *tomodachi* is to be ready to give advice and that of a close friend *(shin'yū)* is to give actual help.

Seniors and Juniors

I mentioned above that people of differing age or social status usually form a relationship which does not fully coincide with normal friendship. The existence of seniority in Japanese society has sometimes been interpreted in an exotic way: the terminology superior/inferior suggests a purely formal and cold hierarchical arrangement in which the superior commands and the inferior defers. This is the reason why in this book the terms senior/junior are preferred. Of course, as in any Western setting, a senior can occasionally be junior by age.

The relation of a senior and a junior can, of course, be a formal relationship and occasionally the boss may be rough or insensitive to the needs of his subordinates. However, it is common that seniors and juniors are what we would call "friends." Their relationship is informal, they are mutually considerate, and they prove to be interested in each other's private affairs. However, it is normally expected that some of the duties and privileges will be exercised in one direction only. For instance, a senior will not normally require the advice of his junior (though he will normally take account of his opinion); when sharing an entertainment situation the senior person will be expected to pay the bill, etc. Like friends, seniors are expected to provide not simply advice but also help in private matters that concern their inferiors. The directionality of the relationship is acknowledged in the Japanese language by a more honorific usage from the junior, and by more "formal" non-verbal behavior (bowing, gestures, tone of voice, etc.). The communicative distance can actually be so large that for a foreign observer it may totally conceal the cordiality of the relationship.

A typical domain in which both the friendship and the senior/junior relationship coexist is the work domain. Japanese offices or companies usually present fairly "friendly" environments. Quite a number of informal entertainment situations are shared. Members of the same company regularly travel together for pleasure and such occasions provide an opportunity to establish friendship and informal relations in general. Of course, it will not be necessary to add that in any domain of human activity there are also seniors who are haughty or undeservedly harsh, juniors who irritate by their incompetence, and colleagues who are lazy and would prefer others to do their work. In this respect, again, there is little difference between Japan and most other societies. An average person has to learn in Japan as anywhere else how to put up with these conditions and how to manage his human relations with the totality of the others.

Patterns of Entertainment

The myth of the Japanese "workaholism" has created the impression that the Japanese work all the time and are unable to participate in normal entertainment situations. There are people who cannot imagine that the Japanese also play sports, are enthusiastic mountain climbers, listen to music, or waste their time in chatting and gossiping. These are normal human occupations for a Japanese as much as for anyone else.

One typical family entertainment activity in urban environments is a Sunday shopping expedition (all major shops are open on Sundays) or a walk in a public park, in each case normally combined with a meal in a restaurant. Eating together is also a very popular form of relaxation for friends. Often this is only a cup of coffee or a drink with people from the same office or company after normal office hours. This custom supports in all major cities an enormous number of restaurants, coffee shops, and various eating and drinking places. The custom developed both because it was unusual to invite friends for a party to one's own house (housing is still one of the sore points of Japanese living conditions) and because people who work together live normally in various directions and at places so distant that it is impractical to meet again once they return home.

After lectures, seminars, and similar occasions, at least some of the participants normally have a cup of coffee or a drink with the speaker. By the way, it may be a shocking experience for a visiting Japanese speaker overseas if everyone just says goodbye and leaves after his lecture without providing an opportunity to "finish up" the situation in a friendly informal encounter.

There are many types of parties. The traditional parties are all "sitting parties" at which refreshments or meals are served, either in the Japanese or Western style, and where participants take turns in making speeches, singing, or similar activities. It is almost certain that if there are speeches or singing, foreign participants will also be asked to contribute. Depending on the purpose of the party it can be, for instance, a *sōbetsukai* (farewell party), *kangeikai* (welcoming party), *konshinkai* (a reunion), *bōnenkai* (end-of-the-year party), or one of many other types. More recently, "standing parties" of the Anglo-Saxon type, at which participants can freely circulate, select their partners, and switch between them during the party, have also become popular. However, a number of Japanese will prefer a party at which they can sit together and enjoy listening to a monologue rather than engaging in conversation.

Eating Together

A few more words will be in place here about the important situation of sharing a meal with your Japanese contacts. There are basically three kinds of food (and corresponding establishments): Western food, Chinese food, and Japanese food.

Western food is available in great variety, especially in Tokyo, and ranges from cheap sandwiches, spaghetti, or hamburgers to an elaborate course in a very expensive French restaurant. Western food is well established and popular — it is an inalienable part of the present-day Japanese culinary culture. Bread is sold everywhere and Tokyo may today be one of the cities with the best bread in the world. Imported beer and wines are widely available, but Japanese beer is generally rated as one of the best in the world and Japanese wines are not as laughable as they were some twenty years ago.

Chinese food is served in cheap cafes at virtually every corner of any town (where the cooks are usually Japanese); in more expensive Chinese restaurants or in very respectable establishments, you can partake of amazing delicacies prepared by the best Japanese and Chinese chefs.

Japanese food (in the sense of "traditional Japanese food") can be divided into three broad categories: (1) elaborate, (2) à la carte, and (3) home-style food. The elaborate type is served in special establishments called *ryōriya*; it is normally very expensive and inaccessible without an introduction and prior reservation; it consists of a whole course of dishes, meticulously prepared, arranged, and served with great taste by attendants dressed in kimonos. The famous Japanese geisha can be described as the highest level of waiting and entertaining personnel in these establishments. Ordinary Japanese men—to say nothing of women—have probably never been to a real *ryōriya* and have never even seen a geisha. *Ryōriya* mainly serve business people who govern large entertainment funds. High-ranking foreigners are sometimes invited and given the opportunity to experience this rather bizarre aspect of Japanese culture.

A somewhat less sophisticated version of this elaborate food is available in Japanese inns (*ryokan*) as the evening meal. Both the *ryōriya* and the inns serve food in a traditional Japanese interior on tatami (mats). The meal is accompanied by Japanese saké or beer. Another variety of the elaborate food is the traditional *kaiseki ryōri*, originally served in connection with the tea ceremony. Today, the term is used more widely and designates Japanese-style banquets, at which, of course, other than vegetarian dishes are served.

The à la carte food is served in normal restaurants, many of them specializing in one genre: there are sushi, tempura, grilled-eel *(unagi)*, pork-cutlet *(tonkatsu)*, and noodle shops, among many others. However, some cheap restaurants located in shopping centers or department stores serve a number of these dishes. The lunch of a Japanese employee, unless he brings his lunch box with him from home or prefers a Western or a Chinese dish, normally consists of one of these à la carte dishes.

Home-style food is often Japanese, but Western and Chinese

cuisines have found their way into this domain as well. The Japanese breakfast is now normally a Western breakfast, with (black) tea or coffee and bread. However, the traditional Japanese breakfast with *miso* (bean-paste) soup and rice still survives. Dinner is now often a mixture of an originally Japanese dish (with fish as its main component) and a Western or Chinese dish (based on meat or vegetables).

There is hardly anything in Japanese food that would present problems to a traveler. Raw fish used to be unusual but is now widely enjoyed by all sophisticated foreigners. Occasionally, there are components such as slices of boiled octopus or a raw egg, which may be less common, but it should console us that some Japanese do not like them either.

Some frequent misunderstandings concern drinks. Japanese green tea is not available in coffee/tea shops at all, and can actually hardly ever be purchased. Of course, it accompanies a Japanese or Chinese meal free of charge. Saké is unavailable in shops that specialize in Western food.

When eating with the Japanese, foreigners are often confused concerning who should pay. If the occasion was quite clearly initiated by the other side, there is no necessity to offer sharing the expenses. This is particularly true when the expenses are likely to be covered from a company or a public entertainment budget. Of course, it will be necessary to say thank you. Otherwise, it is advisable to offer sharing the cost, but to give up if the other person is quite clearly senior. It is the senior person's right to entertain juniors, and it is expected that he will normally accept his responsibility. A Japanese senior will probably take it as an encroachment on his rights if a young foreign visitor attempts to pay the bill. It follows that a foreign professor will be expected to pay for the coffee of his Japanese student.

Travel

As mentioned above, travel with friends or people who work at the same place (normally organized by the employer) is also a very common form of entertainment. This often simply involves staying in a Japanese inn (taking a hot bath, often with other people from the group of the same sex, and sleeping on Japanese mats in the same room) or a hotel, relaxing, and having the evening and morning meals together. Foreign participants on such trips will not be required to share the bath. Occasionally some sightseeing is optionally included. This form of "passive" travel may be unusual in other societies and may become a source of misunderstanding in intercultural contact. Even overseas group travel of the Japanese bears traces of this attitude to traveling.

Foreigners who travel in Japan normally wish to experience a stay in a Japanese inn (*ryokan*). Although this may be more expensive than staying in a Western-style hotel, the experience is important, particularly since this may be the only opportunity to become acquainted with the traditional life on tatami. The principal sources of misunderstanding in a Japanese inn probably concern two matters. One is the rule that shoes or slippers are never worn for walking on tatami. Moreover, it is necessary to change slippers when entering the toilet: staying in a Japanese inn requires therefore constant putting on and taking off of slippers. The second problem is with the Japanese bath. Most *ryokan* provide an opportunity for those who do not wish to use the common bath (with almost no exceptions separate for men and women). It is well known that one lathers up and washes *outside* the bath and enters the tub to warm the body only *after* having washed. Out of consideration for guests who will be using the same bath after you, it is inappropriate to bring the temperature of the water down by adding cold water.

Sports and Hobbies

Foreigners sometimes imagine that either judo or sumo are the national sports of Japan. This is incorrect. The most preferred and most widely practiced sport is unquestionably baseball. Almost every Japanese male has tried to play it and people of both sexes enjoy watching it. It has no social class marker attached to it. Golf is quite clearly an upper- or upper-middle-class sport, because of the considerable expenses involved. Tennis, rugby, soccer, basketball, etc. are rather middle class. Karate and aikido command a lower social prestige than judo. There are also other traditional sports, such as *kendō* (Japanese fencing) which is practiced in many schools, both by boys and by girls. Sumo, the Japanese style of wrestling, is of course extremely popular, and viewed on the TV by enormous numbers of people. However, it is not practiced widely and could therefore be hardly described as the "national sport."

Apart from many internationally shared hobbies, Japanese hobbies include learning some of the traditional cultural genres. Girls attend courses as a part of their preparation for marriage, with ikebana (Japanese flower arrangement), the tea ceremony, *koto* (Japanese harp), and Japanese dancing lessons being among the most popular choices. Nobody expects that the pupils will practice much when they get married. It may be added in this context that almost all of the ikebana and tea ceremony tuition in contemporary Japan caters for this pre-marriage market, and has little existence outside this framework. Calligraphy is very popular among many Japanese, both in its more practical form aiming at neat handwriting (*shūji*), and as an art (*shodō*). Some forms of Japanese singing (*kouta*) and the composition of poems in classical Chinese are pastimes associated normally with the higher level executives in Japanese companies. In their forties and fifties many middle-class women, liberated to a large extent from the duties of looking after their children, take up again the hobbies they learned in their youth and freely add others. Cooking courses, music, study in adult education classes, and of course sports provide a wide range of alternatives from which they can select.

Participation in Popular Culture

One further note should be added here. Most of the Japanese we meet will possess almost all of our own culture and will also have some competence in at least some aspect of the traditional high brow Japanese culture. However, in addition, there are genres of *popular* Japanese culture, not widely known overseas, which may occupy an important place in the person's life. Even if there are Japanese, mainly intellectuals of samurai origin, who are not consumers of Japanese popular culture, it is true that most people enjoy it and that it plays an important place in their life. A university professor of (Western) philosophy, who went to concerts of (Western) classical music regularly, told me recently that he also liked Japanese cartoon books (*manga*), popular historical novels, and listened for pleasure to Japanese popular songs (*kayōkyoku*).

There are many genres of popular culture, some of them of course distributed in sub-sections of the Japanese population only—for instance, among people of rural or urban origin, a particular social class, or people with a particular family tradition. Some of the genres have already been mentioned: *rakugo*, *manzai*, *naniwa-bushi*, *sumō*, etc. A new genre is *karaoke*, singing popular songs, mostly of the *kayōkyoku* type, to pre-recorded instrumental accompaniment.

The vitality of popular culture is enormous and foreigners who wish to establish firm ties with the Japanese are advised to take account of its importance for their contacts.

ECONOMY AND STANDARD OF LIVING

Economic Miracle and the Problem of Communication

In mid-1980s almost sixty million Japanese were working for a living. Out of this number, three-quarters were employees and one-quarter were self-employed or employed within their own family. These figures are very different from those of 1960, when ordinary employees were only slightly more numerous than self-employed or family workers. As a consequence of the Japanese "economic miracle," the character of the Japanese work force has completely changed in less than twenty-five years. Small family enterprises gradually came to play a less and less important role, particularly since the size of the population engaged in agriculture changed. While in 1960, thirty percent of the total work force was active in primary industry (agriculture, forestry, and fishing), in the mid-1980s the figure dropped to less than ten percent. On the other hand, the percentage of people who worked in tertiary industries (commerce, finance, transport, and various services, including public service) rose from forty to more than fifty-five percent. In this respect the structure of employment became very similar to that in other leading industrial countries of the world.

It is of course the Japanese manufacturing industry that has attracted so much attention throughout the world ever since the Japanese "economic miracle" started in the late 1950s. Japan, which until then was for many the nation of unimaginative copy-cats, suddenly came to play a major and innovative role in world economy.

Many tried to explain the phenomenon. However, this is not the place where a summary of arguments could be presented. What is important to realize in the context of this book is that it was to a large extent the "economic miracle" that made the world newly interested in Japan, that brought the Japanese businessmen (and because of the improved economic conditions also tourists, students, and many others) into intensive contact with other countries, and that thus created the contemporary problem of communication.

Japanese Style of Management

However, one aspect of Japanese economy, which is directly related to the way we view the Japanese as individuals, must be mentioned here: the issue of the Japanese style of management. Many of the Japanese we meet are working in companies or other similar organizations. Without understanding the basic character of their working life we can hardly achieve much real understanding when we communicate with them.

Much has been said and written on this subject and it has been emphasized that the system is very different from the usual Western practice. It has often been claimed that Japanese management is based on a number of unique factors: life-long employment, a specific seniority system, enterprise unions, fostering of group identity, and a number of welfare measures adopted by employers. The Japanese system of management has often been hailed as one which should be emulated overseas.

It is necessary to say in this context that a number of scholars engaged in the study of Japanese labor relations have more recently adopted a position that does not overrate the differences. They have suggested that the quoted features of the Japanese system may actually not be quite that unique; they have also expressed doubts about the efficiency of others. Furthermore, serious doubts have been expressed with regard to the possibility of application of Japanese management techniques in other societies. Many Japanese executives will speak with pride about the system and are likely to possess no doubts about its uniqueness and qualities. Nevertheless, a number of companies are actually developing their management in a direction which resembles modern Western models: the principle of life-long employment is receiving lesser prominence, seniority tends to be based more on competence than on the length of service, and the direct ideological pressure on employees is decreasing.

One of the facts that frequently remains unmentioned by those who admire the system is the limitation of the quoted characteristics to large Japanese companies, which do not employ among themselves more than twenty percent of the work force. This is likely to cover the majority of Japanese executives we meet overseas. However, most Japanese employees work under much less favorable conditions and the efficiency of many small- or medium-scale enterprises is less than satisfactory. Neither is it true that Japanese governmental and other offices of governmental or semi-governmental enterprises (e.g., the former Japanese National Railways, etc.) could serve as examples of ideal working conditions or efficiency.

When foreign visitors observe a Japanese company in action, a number of unusual features is likely to attract their attention. One is the large room (ōbeya) in which most of the office personnel are located. A section head (kachō) usually occupies a desk from behind which he can see his subordinates. A settee and easy chairs are likely to be located in his area and serve as the place where visitors are accepted, except when special consultation rooms are available on one side of the large room. A departmental head (buchō) usually has a separate room, sometimes created by a glass partition at one end of the large room.

While watching the polite behavior of personnel when they approach section and departmental heads (bowing, ceremonial handing over of documents, standing in attention, etc.), foreign observers easily misinterpret the actual situation within the organization. The superior may be the real boss, but it may also be that he is only putting his seal on letters—seals are used instead of signatures—after decisions have been made by others in the company. The reverential attitude, though not as strong as it may appear, is genuine, but it does not necessarily reflect the relationship of power within the company.

Whereas Western organizations are usually strongly hierarchical, with the boss deciding about any matter of importance, in Japan the decision usually takes into account the views of more than one person. Some may be directly consulted, while the position of others, if known, may only be taken into account in an indirect way. All issues are thoroughly talked over in informal networks (*nemawashi*) before a decision is formalized at a formal gathering or in a circular, called *ringisho*, to which personnel at various levels and in various departments concerned attach their final comments and personal seals. In any case, people in subordinate positions will consider carefully what their superiors and colleagues will deem to be the proper action. Superiors will take into account the opinion of their subordinates.

The best procedure for foreigners to follow is normally to obtain an introduction to a person who is highly situated in the organization, secure an overall authorization for further negotiations, and then work out details of the proposal with less senior personnel. On the whole, it is very important what the person who is actually dealing with the case, however lowly situated within the company he may be, thinks about it. This is an important point for foreigners to remember. Superiors are often unfamiliar with details of individual cases and happily rely on the way they are presented to them by their subordinates.

Employees often stay after office hours and sometimes actually continue working. However, this is not always the case. The overtime hours may be spent in social contact or in informal discussions connected with work in general. This is one of the occasions when information concerning the company, the area in which it is active, and economy in general, flows in all directions. The Japanese society is an information-hungry society. Perhaps that is one of the major components of the Japanese success.

Standard of Living

The times when foreigners looked at Japan as a poor Asian country are over. The Japanese are among the world's biggest spenders, not only when they travel overseas but also at home. Consumer expenditure is as high as in Western Europe or higher. People in Japan have experienced considerable growth in the standard of living since World War II and in particular in the last twenty years. There is no doubt that the standard of consumption in contemporary Japan is very high. Of course, this continued rise is reflected in the attitude of those Japanese who are doing well even in their discussions about Japan with foreigners. Many people in contemporary Japan believe that since Japan's GNP is second only to that of the USA, so is the standard of living.

However, some negative features of the Japanese way of living can be easily detected by any visitor to the country. The standard of housing is still very poor, even if admittedly much better than a decade ago. Housing is very expensive, too, because low-cost loans are not readily available. The lack of public investment in the past is visible. Roads and pavements, lighting, arrangements for garbage, the state of public conveniences, and many other aspects of life in the large Japanese cities are far from being satisfactory. Public transport in major Japanese cities may be very effective, but to travel to and from work in the peak hours is certainly not a pleasant experience, in particular if we realize that the average commuting time for a Tokyo company employee is approximately three hours. Transfer from one place to another in Tokyo, with its numerous pedestrian bridges and subways, may be all right for young people but can present considerable problems for the aged. Health services are effective and relatively cheap, but the facilities are not necessarily nice and clean and there may be little personal attention. Only a small percentage of households is connected to sewerage. In all these areas large amounts of investment will be necessary to bring the quality of life close to the level of the rich Western nations. However, in view of the general upward trend in the Japanese economy, problems like this are not always noted in Japan.

There are also other aspects of the not-so-rich Japan that may escape the attention of a visitor. One of them is the overcrowding of schools. Again, much larger budgets will be necessary if the aim of individual attention to each student is to be attained.

Japan is a typical consumer society and many Japanese who possess the experience of living overseas simply compare the availability and range of choice in consumer goods. This, of course, in Japan is enormous, and second to no other country. Also, some services are very well developed. However, many Japanese who know life in other developed countries would prefer to live overseas, not merely because it might be more interesting, but also because they feel that overseas life is in many respects more convenient than life in Japan.

JAPAN AND THE WORLD

Japanese Businessmen Overseas

One of the dreams of any young Japanese joining the work force some twenty years ago was to be posted overseas. Now, the opportunity to travel overseas and to work in an overseas office of one's company have increased radically, and working outside of Japan has become quite common. Rather than being posted "overseas" in general, the question is where? Some countries or areas are much preferred to others. Among the developed countries it is those with the highest standards of living that are most popular. However, there are people who prefer interesting work to easy living, and may be happy when posted to the Near East or to a Southeast Asian country.

All major economic centers of the world and many other large cities host extensive communities of Japanese businessmen and employees of other Japanese organizations. Accusations of creating closed networks, consisting purely of the Japanese, have been frequently made, and it must be admitted that the Japanese communities tend to limit many activities to members of their own ethnic group.

However, the issue should be considered with calm and without bias. First of all, let us realize that in most cases it is not the Japanese alone who behave in this way. Many other foreign groups do. For one thing, consider the foreign community in Japan. Is it totally open to the Japanese? Do foreigners living in Japan always seek participation in purely Japanese networks? It seems that the world is not prepared for a totally free mixing of various ethnic groups. The process may be relatively advanced, but it is far from being completed.

Another factor to consider is the amount of communication problems which the Japanese face in comparison with many other foreign communities. More will be said about this problem in the following chapter. Finally, those who criticize the Japanese (or any other ethnic group for that matter) should realize that free mixing with the host community is a matter which requires two sides: the foreign and the local. However, the local communities, in the First, Second, or in the Third Worlds may not be very keen on accepting new members. It is simply not true that all social networks in America, Australia, England, France, Jordan, or the Philippines have an unlimited number of vacancies. When there is a vacancy, it is likely to be filled with someone who is not deviant from the point of view of the culture in question. People who possess a culture as distant from most others as the Japanese do not frequently get a chance.

One of the problems unparalleled in any other ethnic community of expatriates is the problem of the education of children. Because of company circumstances or because of problems with obtaining long-term visas, most members of the Japanese community are relatively short-term residents, with an average period of stay of approximately three years. The children of these Japanese families have transferred from a Japanese school and will return to a Japanese school when the family returns to Japan. If they attend the local school, it is more than likely that they will get radically behind in the acquisition of Japanese characters. This acquisition, which requires a considerable amount of time and effort, is a task of a completely different magnitude and type from learning to read and write in German or in French. Also, the "difficult" vocabulary is much more extensive in Japanese than in the Western languages. The adaptation of Japanese children after a sojourn overseas back to a Japanese school has proved to be a serious problem. No wonder that, sometimes with considerable hesitation, a number of Japanese communities overseas have opted for a fully Japanese school rather than for the local school on weekdays followed by short courses on weekends or in the evenings.

Tourists and Students

Apart from the businessman, the typical Japanese who can be encountered overseas are tourists. There are of course people who travel individually, and their number seems to be on the increase, but most undertake their trips in groups organized by travel agents. This fact has sometimes been taken for proof of the alleged Japanese trend for "group orientation." However, why should people who mostly possess no command of a foreign language and no previous experience of foreign travel be deprived of the convenience of traveling with a guide and with all arrangements made on their behalf? The matter is further complicated by the fact that owing to the pattern of travel for relaxation within Japan, mentioned above, even the average Japanese expects to stay in very good hotels. However, adequate information concerning hotels is not easily available to individual travelers. It is subject to doubt whether unorganized individual travel really provides a much more worthwhile experience than group travel. Of course, in the case of group travel, there may be no direct contact with the local population at all. However, unless they meet friends and talk extensively to casual acquaintances, individual travelers may not derive much pleasure or benefit from meeting the local people either. All they do is to buy tickets, pay for food, or look for a suitable hotel room.

The number of Japanese students overseas has also increased. Exchange schemes exist in the case of many countries, and there are many private students, particularly at colleges and universities. Many problems enountered by Japanese students are of a communicative nature, of misunderstood personality and intentions. It is difficult to initiate and maintain friendship and to relate successfully to other students of the opposite sex. However, Japanese students also face problems which result from differences in the educational system and even the best may need considerable time to adjust.

Emigrants

The rise in imporance of the above categories has somehow made the question of Japanese emigrants less prominent. The prewar emigration was particularly strong to Hawaii, California, and some South American countries, such as Brazil. However, with the emigrants being now in their third or fourth generation, their assimilation has proceeded to a considerable extent and competence in the Japanese language tends to be lost. Postwar emigration has been very limited in extent. There are many Japanese women in countries such as the USA and Australia who married allied servicemen and live with their families overseas. Apart from that there are individuals, but on the whole the Japanese are not at present an ethnic group that tends to emigrate in large numbers. It may be noted that in many cases the new communities of businessmen face the Japanese "war brides" with some hesitation. While the former are middle class and well educated, the latter are normally not. Sometimes they speak a regionally marked variety of Japanese and occasionally are in the process of losing the ability to use the language. A similar attitude used to be applied to second-generation Japanese, who spoke a Japanese learned from their parents, that was regionally marked, informal, and sometimes inadequate. However, contemporary Japanese are much more prepared to accept the fact that people with Japanese-sounding names are actually not Japanese at all.

Perception of the Japanese by Overseas Academics

It is good to realize that there are many ways of approaching the problem of the Japanese in the academic world, in the mass media, and by the ordinary people in Western countries. A number of images and attitudes result.

The way of looking at Japan in the oldest academic system of perceiving Japanese culture, in the "Japanology paradigm," was ambivalent. On one hand, there was a great admiration for traditional Japan. This was connected with conceiving of Japan as a basically exotic place, full of colorful and inscrutable but rich culture. On the other hand, for these academics everything new in Japan was interpreted as a corruption of the genuine Japanese culture and despised. Any achievement in modern culture was "copying the West" and hardly worth noticing. This view of Japan is out of fashion now, but occasionally still survives. Various cultural programs of Japanese governmental organizations, directed towards overseas markets, have supported this kind of perception.

In the following historical period, academics obtained more direct experience of Japan. However, this experience was still insufficient to provide them with a realistic assessment. The exotic character of Japan was not emphasized any more. Instead academics became interested in the Westernization of Japan. The problem was how to bring Japan in line with their own societies. The complaint against Japan was now not that it was "copying," or Westernizing too much, but that it was not "Westernizing" (modernizing) enough. For this perception, various features of Japanese culture or society which were different from those of the West (e.g., features of the family, education, company, etc.) were labeled as "premodern" and predestined for removal. The conviction that Japan possesses a unique (premodern) structure, that the Japanese are "group oriented," and that they prefer hierarchical social structures all belong to this period.

It is only in the third, contemporary, approach that a more relaxed attitude toward Japan started asserting itself. Japan experts of this period are for the first time people who possess an intimate knowledge of the society. Japan is neither exotic nor premodern for them. It is a society like any other. If asked whether the Japanese are good or bad people, they will laugh. Of course, some people are good and some people are bad. Variation among the Japanese is fully accepted. So is the fact of conflict in the society. There are a number of negative features of Japan, such as mentioned in the previous text. Academics who think in this third paradigm do not divide the world so clearly into "them" (the Japanese) and "us." Japan is observed from the inside, not as an extraneous phenomenon.

Mass Media Perceptions of Japan

The situation in the mass media of the West is still unsatisfactory. Although there are exceptions, in particular among journalists who work in Japan, the general trend seems to be to find a simple principle which would explain all. Informed by academics belonging to the second group mentioned above, the journalists often find the all-explanatory principle in what has been called the "premodern" features, such as the assumed trend to act in groups or to establish hierarchies. In their approach to Japan such people often move between two extremes: on one hand, an unlimited admiration; on the other, criticism that is too extensive and unjust.

Japan as Perceived by the Average Citizen

A number of public opinion surveys have recently been conducted to find out what the images of Japan of the average citizens are. There seems to be considerable amount of variation and it may perhaps lack justification if I attempt a summary. On the whole these surveys show that the immediately preceding historical period in which Japan acted with considerable arrogance and brutality, attempting to steal through aggressive military policies from the Western powers their political and economic domination of Asia, still remains a source of negative evaluation of Japan and the

Japanese. The fact, noted above, that most Japanese did accept responsibility for their behavior in the course of World War II and the preceding period, and that this history is not likely to repeat itself, has not been noted with sufficient clarity. Of course, actions of some sections of Japanese society, such as the recent revision by the Ministry of Education of textbooks, in which the war was portrayed in a way unacceptable to the Asian nations that had suffered, act as a factor bringing the war issue back onto the scene. Much will depend in the future on the attitudes of the Japanese companies that are active overseas. Will they confirm the theory already suggested by some, that they merely represent a new form of agression? Or will they succeed in creating the image that they are active overseas not merely for their own benefit but also for the benefit of the countries involved?

The public opinion surveys also show that the flow of information from Japan overseas, though very limited, has succeeded in creating new misunderstandings. The old image of the geisha-samurai Japanese is quickly disappearing. However, it is being replaced by the image of a hardworking and efficient race, people who are packed into overcrowded cities, form a secret clique of their own, people who take orders easily, and who cannot be trusted. More recently, the fear of "new nationalism" has been included. Apart from the reminiscence of the war, this image quite clearly results from factors such as the economic power of Japan, the presence of Japanese goods, the stereotypes of the Japanese society which emphasize groupism and hierarchy, and the fact that some of the Japanese who have been met, if there were any, did not succeed in communicating that they are people like anyone else, people who have their problems, but who are basically kind, polite, and who like to laugh.

What is needed in our own approach to Japan is simply realism. Japan should be neither beautified nor sneered at. Like all other societies, it has many shortcomings. Its people have also achieved results which they are justly proud of. All this must be accepted. Unless we do recognize that the Japanese are basically the same people as we are (whoever "we" may be), even though superb methods for the study of the Japanese language and communication patterns may be developed, communication with the Japanese is still not likely to improve.

THREE
RULES OF COMMUNICATION

In Chapter One the term communicative competence was introduced to account for a vast area of behavior that is neither "linguistic" in the usual narrow sense of the word (since it does not pertain to grammar, pronunciation, vocabulary, or script) nor "cultural" in the sense this word normally possesses. Communicative competence refers to the middle ground between language and culture: it includes rules that are clearly rules of communication, but that are not normally accounted for in the study of "language." On the other hand, to maintain that they are rules of culture like any other rules of daily life, social or cultural conduct, or thought would result in stripping them of their specific character and role in communication. A preliminary survey of the types of such rules was offered in Chapter One.

COMMUNICATION RULES IN JAPAN

A Lunch with Miss Watanabe

Let me use an example to summarize the range of communication rules. Suppose that you want to take Miss Watanabe, a music teacher, to lunch. In the process of inviting her, both you and Miss Watanabe employ a considerable number of rules of communicative competence. Firstly, there is the question whether to formally invite her or not. The decision to communicate your invitation may appear to naturally follow, once you have made up your mind. It cannot be denied that an urge to transfer information normally *switches on* a communication act. However, sometimes our communication rules may prescribe or advise against switching on an act of communication. For instance, although invitations are common in Japan, in some instances people will hesitate to issue an explicit invitation, even if they have clearly decided to invite you. An explicit invitation may sound too presumptuous and a much better way may be to steer the situation which precedes the lunch in such a way that eating together looks like a "happening." In our case, Miss Watanabe will probably not mind being explicity invited. She knows that sometimes the lack of communication may lead to a misunderstanding: tables may be booked or food cooked, and no guests available. This is what actually happens in contact situations.

Once you have decided to communicate to Miss Watanabe your invitation, the next choice is that of the appropriate *language* (variety of language). Since you cannot speak Japanese, the invitation will be issued in English. However, the selection also includes a more detailed question of the level of language you use. You may not be quite aware of the fact that you will probably select an informal (rather than a formal) variety of English. However, since Miss Watanabe's English is not perfect, you are likely to speak carefully and may move your language up on the scale of formality. However, if overdone, your "foreigner talk" might offend Miss Watanabe.

The time you have reached your decision is approximately 8 o'clock in the evening. Is it all right to ring her at home? Your communication *setting* rules specify when and where you are allowed to initiate communication. You have only met Miss Watanabe the day before and she gave you her home number; however, you feel that you do not know her well enough to use her home telephone, especially at this relatively advanced time of the evening. Your rules of communicative competence will probably guide you not to proceed until the next morning. Of course, the relevant rules are different in the case of Japanese: as a matter of fact it is quite all right to call people at their home number until at least 8 or 9 P.M. This applies even to people one does not know well.

Who should you talk to tomorrow? You can of course speak to Miss Watanabe directly, but if she is absent, is it correct to leave a message with her colleague? Or should you call Mrs. Satō, who brought you together and who seemed to be very close to Miss Watanabe? Perhaps she might join in the lunch. In other words, you face a decision about whom it is appropriate to involve in issuing the invitation. The rules of communication you use here will be referred to below as *participant* rules.

With regard to *content*, too, a number of rules must be applied. An invitation in English normally contains information about time, place, and the fact that a meal will be served. Since the use of the word "lunch" would be a little formal, you will try to circumscribe; however, this may make the communication of your intention difficult and in view of Miss Watanabe's reduced competence in English you may decide to violate your variety rule and be informal, rather than risk a misunderstanding. In the case of invitations, some information usually remains uncommunicated. For instance, you do not specify when the lunch would finish. This may be mentioned on a printed invitation for a cocktail party, but it would be unusual to specify it for a lunch or a dinner. Actually, Miss Watanabe might like to know: she has the experience that in different countries lunch can finish at different times. In Japan, people can stay quite long. Another matter which often remains uncommunicated in English is who other guests are. In Japan, by the way, no similar constraint is valid and your host may tell you the names of all other people who have been invited.

Once you know what the content of your invitation will be, you decide about the way in which the *message* through which you communicate will be arranged and how certain "prefabricated" components will be used. First, the invitation cannot be the only part of your conversation on the occasion. You know that conversations in Japanese obligatorily commence with a formalized reference to your previous meeting, and you wonder whether this should also apply in this case. In English the invitation itself normally starts with a check whether the invitee is free at the scheduled time, and then proceeds toward other details, closing with an assurance that both sides are looking forward to the occasion. A number of half-fixed routine expressions are applied in the course of this converation. For instance, the only reason that can be given to decline an invitation is a previous engagement, and native speakers of English know how to utter the relevant phrases. However, there is no similar routinized statement in Japanese and native speakers of Japanese can sometimes hesitate too much, or use an excuse which is unacceptable from the point of view of English.

The medium you selected for communicating the invitation is the spoken language as used over the telephone. The fact that the use of telephone for the given purpose is appropriate in both English and Japanese is not self-evident. One has to know. For instance, for serious apologies the telephone is normally unsuitable in Japanese. Other possible channels of communication would have been the direct spoken channel—you could have gone to see Miss Watanabe to communicate your intention—or you could have sent a letter. Of course, an invitation which would use printed cards is very formal nowadays and in your case is out of the question either in English or in Japanese; however, a scribbled note would be all right. Decisions of this type will be discussed here under the label *channel* rules.

Rules of Communication

As we have just seen, even a simple speech act such as an invitation for lunch is subject to a large number of rules, some of them perhaps conscious, but most used in an unconscious way. The example given above should be sufficient to prove that speakers act according to rules and apply them in speech situations. The rules are not universal. They vary in different systems of communication, and a possibility of communication problems due to the application of such rules is a real one. This chapter suggests how to avoid some of such problems.

In a system which is derived from the theory of the "ethnography of communication" of Dell Hymes, the rules of communication can be named as follows:

1. Switch-on rules (under what conditions?)
2. Variety rules (in what "language?")
3. Setting rules (when and where?)
4. Participant rules (who?)
5. Content rules (what?)
6. Message rules (in what form?)
7. Channel rules (through what medium?)
8. Management rules

These last are used to label speech, evaluate it, and improve it if it has been found in some way deficient.

The way in which the rules have been presented above might seem to imply that they are applied in the order in which they have been discussed. This is not the case. In the process of the creation of speech, speakers constantly move forward and backward, and return to change their previous decisions. The issue of the order of application of rules is thus a complicated one and cannot be discussed in this book.

Communication rules have only become the object of systematic study approximately two decades ago. In comparison with the rules of language, which have been studied for centuries, we know very little about them and to attempt a full systematic account of the Japanese rules would be premature. This book does not pretend to provide a systematic picture of communication: illustrations are merely drawn to stimulate understanding and further interest.

Variation in Communication Rules

However, before we start with the discussion of individual rules of communication, it will not be out of place to emphasize one important point. In the same way as variation exists in society, there is also variation in the communication system. When in this chapter Japanese communication is mentioned, it must be understood that different people communicate differently. This does not imply that each speaker communicates in a completely individual way. However, speakers from varying parts of the community may show considerable variation in the use of language. Although no detailed studies exist on the subject, the distinctions are clearly perceived by native speakers. According to the popular stereotype, Kantō and Kansai speakers adhere to somewhat different rules. So do speakers from urban and rural areas. Similar differences exist in most societies and should not surprise us. Of course, social class distinctions are also pervasive, age is an important factor, and women communicate differently from men. Again, all this happens in our own societies as well, except that when we observe a foreign society as distant from us as Japan, the differences may be more difficult to see or may appear to be of lesser importance.

In this book we shall take the point of view of those Japanese whom foreigners are most likely to meet first: the middle-class people of the Tokyo area. Particularly outstanding differences will be mentioned in the text.

SWITCH-ON RULES:
WHAT THE CONDITIONS
OF COMMUNICATION ARE

It is not true that people communicate whatever comes to their mind. Only a small part of our observations and attitudes are verbalized. It would also be incorrect to assume that whether we decide to talk or remain silent is governed by universal rules that are the same in all societies. In the older types of Western societies there was a rule that "children should be seen but not heard," and some readers may remember the operation of this rule in their own experience. In the contemporary industrial societies of the West, this rule has certainly been dropped and is not valid any more. Communication rules change and vary in our own society. We should be prepared to accept that they also vary between our society and Japan.

Talking More or Less?

It may be an exaggeration to say that in Japanese speech is switched on less often than in English. However, this exaggeration may explain behavior in contact situations which often puzzles foreigners. First, there is a rule that when a clearly senior speaker is present, the right to initiate speech stays with him. It is in particularly bad taste to bombard him with questions, and to try to engage him in conversation against his wish. Hence, unless the superior initiates speech, silence may be appropriate. Admittedly, this rule can be described as conservative, and is not necessarily adhered to by all.

Further, speech is sometimes less easily initiated when the communication network consists of "out-group" speakers who are not friends or well known to each other. Although some speakers manage in these situations perfectly well, the less communicatively skilled do not. For example, some Japanese exchange students who have just arrived overseas can manage to communicate well in situations in which they are not yet well acquainted with all participants, but until they feel that they have joined as "in-group" members, many feel communicatively inhibited; they remain silent, however much their hosts may try to "make them speak." Of course, similar situations may occur in many societies. If the rule is different in Japan, the difference is only a matter of degree.

Thirdly, sex differences play a role. It is easier to start communication within the confines of the same sex, rather than across sex boundaries. Japanese exchange students find it often difficult to speak with overseas students of the opposite sex. Foreign adults may possess some experience with regard to drawing the wife of a senior Japanese academic or businessman into the conversation. She spoke better English than her husband, but showed a much more limited amount of conversational activity. This happened even when the topics of conversation were very general ones. Moreover, she may have spoken much more when she was alone with your wife. Again, the examples given above are of students or older people. However, even within these two categories many will feel no constraints on speaking at all.

Fourthly, some situations of daily life are not interpreted as strongly as speech situations as in English. Take for instance a simple lunch in a company canteen during the lunch break. Of course, people will normally speak before and after their meal, but they may remain silent while eating. When this happens in a contact situation—and it will not happen on all occasions—foreigners sometimes hesitate: why is their Japanese partner suddenly so quiet: has he got some particular health problem; or is he angry about some remark made previously in the conversation? The explanation may be simpler than that. The situation is for him primarily one of eating; it is not a speech situation.

Fifthly, in the more conservative idiom of speech, larger groups of people—as I shall explain in detail later—do not break up easily into smaller ones. When you are in a group of five or six people and one of them speaks, it may be difficult to separate out one particular individual from the group to talk to him. He will feel obliged to listen to the person who is talking at the moment, in particular when that person is a senior. If this happens to you, you should understand that the unwillingness to talk of the person you addressed has nothing to do with you personally. He is simply following his own communication rules. If the person you address does talk to you, he may either have broken the rules (which would be relatively easy in a contact situation), or may not have possessed those rules at all. Indeed, many speakers who are not "communicatively conservative" do not hesitate in similar situations at all and will engage in conversation on a one-to-one basis.

Finally, in Japan there is less obligation to talk in situations in which there is little or nothing to say. We do not often realize that such situations are many: the bus stop meeting with a casual acquaintance is a typical case. Most occasions called "parties" also belong to this category. Whenever such a situation occurs, a topic is selected from a range of topics we keep prepared for the occasion. In general, one can say that in many societies we have been educated in the belief that it is wrong not to talk when we are with someone else. But is this belief correct? After all, is it not more rational to speak only when there is a definite message to convey?

While Japanese speakers may frequently undercommunicate, the opposite of course happens in the case of foreign speakers. In the situations outlined above they may violate the Japanese rules by questioning superiors or talking too much in out-group networks; they may be misunderstood when speaking too much and too freely to persons of the opposite sex, asking too many questions over lunch, or trying to split a network in which someone talks, and when talking too much in pure contact situations (the bus stop situation, etc.).

In all the instances discussed above, Japanese speakers communicated less because they followed their own rules of communication. However, interference of the native system is not the only source of problems. In Chapter One noted that another source is "simplification," the inability of speakers to handle too many new rules of culture, communication, and language. In the case of "simplification," Japanese speakers may again talk too little or avoid speech or, on the contrary, they may talk too much. Both of these extremes do occur in contact situations frequently. Of course, they will also occur to foreign speakers of Japanese in situations in which they use the language.

The Duty to Cooperate

H. P. Grice turned our attention to the existence of a very general principle of conversation adhered to in all languages: by taking part in conversation, speakers accept the obligation to cooperatate with each other to develop the communication encounter. They *must* speak. However, foreigners in contact situations often violate the cooperation principle.

For example, each speaker is obliged to take turns in conversation and thus make a contribution. When the topic of Japanese education is discussed, participants develop it by presenting in turn their own experience and comments. When the topic is finished, a new topic must be selected, and those who did not provide a topic previously will normally be expected to do so. However, foreign participants are often unable to perform their duty. Too many rules must be attended to, and speaking may bring discomfort rather then enjoyment, especially if the interlocutor is someone unknown to the speaker. They just sit or stand and watch. In contact situations this is often interpreted as an indication that they do not wish to speak and are avoiding participation in the encounter.

The problem extends. The requirement to cooperate does not cover only the provision of topics but also the extent of participation in general. When a question is asked, it does not suffice to answer "yes" or "no." More than that is required. However, when we speak a foreign language we do very often limit our replies to very short sentences, which give our partners the impression that we do not really want to speak.

Total avoidance of speech is a very frequent phenomenon in contact situations. I remember student parties in Australia at which Australian and Japanese participants were expected to communicate in English. Almost all Japanese students wanted to serve food and drinks, because that gave them the opportunity to participate without engaging in English conversation. Of course, avoidance often affects whole encounters. When we face the task of speaking a language we do not know well, we may decide not to attend. Refusals to accept invitations to parties are examples of acts of avoidance motivated by the fear of communication problems.

Cooperation and Letter Writing

However serious the failure to switch conversation on may be, it is not the only problem of cooperation in communication. In writing, too, people do not cooperate as much as they are expected. A typical case is that of letters. After a trip overseas you are expected to write a letter of thanks to each overseas contact who extended to you more than the usual amount of kindness. If such letters remain unwritten, this is due to the fact that to write a letter in a foreign language is not normally an enjoyable duty. Although, it must be said, some people like it. If you do not, don't hesitate and write to your Japanese contacts in English. Actually many people in Japan will prefer the opportunity to exercise their English competence rather than decipher your sometimes faltering Japanese.

Once a friend brought to me a letter in English from her pen friend in Japan. Something was written at the end in Japanese that was obviously not a part of the letter itself. She wanted to know what it meant. The sentence said: "Jenny, you complain that I write so little to you. Do you realize that to write the page above in English took me six hours to complete?" Jenny's Japanese pen friend apparently wrote this postscript as an expression of his frustration, without dreaming that it would ever be read.

When communication is switched on in a situation in which we would not expect it in our own system of communication, we are surprised and seek an explanation. An American who himself writes letters only when there is a need to convey a message or ask for a favor, was puzzled by a letter from his Japanese friend, which talked much about the weather in Japan and recent family developments, but had no overt message to convey. What did he mean? Was this a gentle way of reminding of a promise, made and forgotten, to render a service? Yes, there was a half-promise, but what was it? The meaning of the act was completely different. As in many other languages, or perhaps more, in Japanese people often write letters to each other without really having much to convey: as a friendly gesture, to reinforce the relationship, show kindness, and sometimes admittedly to practice English composition or Japanese calligraphy.

Diaries and Taking Notes

In Europe and America it used to be common to write diaries. I hope that I do not exaggerate if I say that to write a diary today is rather more a personal habit than a generally accepted pattern. In Japan, bookshops and stationary shops display at the end of the calendar year a large variety of diary books. Many young people keep diaries and when we find out we are sometimes surprised. Some people may interpret this as taking notes on others for clandestine ends.

A diary is an act of communication which is not directed to anyone else. The only addressee is the writer himself. Other communicative acts like that are in most Western societies limited to the necessary minimum, too. For instance, it is not generally required that you take notes at public lectures or business meetings, unless there is really an important point which must not be forgotten. In Japan, to take notes in most situations when someone else is providing an explanation is common. If there is a visitor from Japan who gives a talk, and all foreign participants sit there, looking straight into his eyes, with arms crossed, he may feel rejected and frustrated. It is polite to take notes. All those who travel to Japan, and students who listen to lectures, should take a course in the systematic taking of notes. What you do with the notes afterwards is completely a matter of your own choice.

VARIETY RULES:
WHAT TYPE OF LANGUAGE IS USED

The term ''variety of language'' has been used in linguistics to refer to any ''kind'' of language such as English, Japanese, a dialect of English or Japanese, spoken language (i.e., language used in speaking), or written language (i.e., language used in writing), language used in in-group or out-group encounters, the language of humor, etc. When we communicate we select a variety or a particular mixture of varieties for the situation. Hence, the repertoire of varieties available within a particular community is an important fact in communication.

Varieties of Japanese

A common stereotypical portrait of Japan shows an ethnically and linguistically homogeneous society, but the reality is not as simple as that.

Firstly, the Japanese language itself is not a single entity. More details about variation within Japanese will be presented in the next chapter. Here it will suffice to say that quite an intricate system of choices for the use of language exists. In speaking one must choose between the Standard, the Common Language, and a dialect. The matter is of considerable importance for foreign speakers. Almost all textbooks of Japanese teach the Standard, but in casual conversation the Standard is seldom selected. The Common Language and dialects prevail. The Common Language is close to the Standard, but it contains a number of dialectal features.

In writing, the Standard is the dominant variety, but Common Language and dialects appear whenever spoken language is mirrored in writing (as in dialogues in a novel). Historically flavored language is common in historical novels and in a number of popular songs, school songs, etc. There is enormous variation in the Standard, with the language of law, administration, and politics being the most difficult styles. Some legal codes are written in so-called Classical Japanese which is a language totally different from the varieties of the contemporary Standard. An introductory textbook for foreigners does not normally include more than a very basic and simple form of the written Standard language.

Foreigners who employ Japanese personnel often show little sensitivity to the variation in language. The Japanese public, whether we agree or not, does expect that certain varieties of Japanese, and not others, will be used. For recording messages on tape or for speaking through the microphone (in the case of guides, etc.), impeccable Standard is required. Traces of regional accent may be excused in the case of receptionists who can otherwise handle honorific speech without failure. It is necessary to carefully check whether the applicant for a position in which direct contact with customers is required, has in fact acquired the range of honorifics expected for the job. This is not necessarily guaranteed for all native speakers, even if born and educated in Japan. Some second-generation Japanese who were educated overseas or former exchange students speak excellent Japanese. However, others may only speak a very informal variety which embarrasses or insults less tolerant Japanese speakers.

Foreign employers sometimes assume that any Japanese speaker with good English will be able to produce translations into Japanese which could be printed straight away. This expectation, again, is highly unrealistic. Even if the standards of writing are in general higher among Japanese graduates than among graduates in some English-speaking countries, the range of written styles they can actively use is necessarily limited.

The Ainu Language

Whatever the theory of ethnic and linguistic homogeneity of Japan may claim, varieties of Japanese are not the only varieties of language present in Japan. The other languages which must be given due consideration are Ainu, Korean, Chinese, and English.

I have already mentioned that the position of the Ainu in Japan is unique. Although the number of people who register as of Ainu parentage is small, this is the aboriginal language and culture of Japan. Historically, the Ainu language is remote from Japanese, even if a possibility of common origin exists. At the beginning of the Meiji era, the Ainu still inhabited the whole of the island of Hokkaidō. Today, the language has gone out of use in conversation almost entirely and no support is available for salvaging whatever remains. Many of the people who consider themselves ethnically Ainu would like to learn their language—if not for other reasons then as a symbol of their ethnic identity. However, virtually no facilities exist.

The Korean Language

The situation of Korean in Japan is both similar and different. Similar is the fact of gradual assimilation of the Korean language and its replacement in the younger generation of Koreans by Japanese. Also similar is the lack of support for the maintenance of the language. However, the Korean minority, more numerous and economically stronger than the Ainu, has been able to provide some schooling facilities of its own. The historical background of the Koreans in Japan is also different. At the beginning of Japan's history the Chinese culture came to Japan through the mediation of the Koreans. Korean teachers and artisans lived in Japan and left their distinct mark. However, between this period and the new wave of Korean immigration something like a thousand years elapsed. After Japan annexed Korea in 1910 Korean workers started coming to Japan, voluntarily or as forced labor, and after World War II many of them remained. Although some repatriated later, there are still more than 600,000 people who live in Japan.

The Korean language is linguistically very close to Japanese. Many linguists now believe that it has common parentage with Japanese, although the separation of the two languages must have happened a long time ago and no easily recognizable traces of the relationship remain. However, the grammatical structure of the two languages is extremely similar, and this fact makes the acquisition of Japanese by the Koreans and Korean by the Japanese relatively easy. Koreans in South Korea also use the same Chinese characters as the Japanese, but in North Korea the use of characters has been discontinued.

However similar the grammatical structure of Japanese and Korean may be, the pronunciation is different. In Korean the distinction between k and g, t and d, p and b and similar pairs of consonants, as in Chinese (or German), relies on so called "aspiration" rather than on "voicing," as in Japanese (or French). The result is that when a first-generation Korean speaks Japanese, his g, d, b, etc. often sound like k, t, p, etc. This and other features have often been ridiculed and became a support for discrimintion. Today, or course, the majority of Koreans in Japan are second- or third-generation residents born and educated in Japan, and the concern these people have is rather how to maintain their competence in Korean. Under the present situation of no governmental support for the language, the competence is quickly deteriorating.

Although there is a strong Korean minority in Japan and although Korea, formerly occupied by Japan, is geographically closest to Japan, very few Japanese have learned Korean, even if some interest has appeared in recent years when NHK started broadcasting a course in Korean conversation.

The Chinese Language

The Chinese minority, as already mentioned, is dispersed, and although their competence in Chinese (dialects) is maintained, it has neither the symbolic importance of Ainu, nor the political importance of Korean. However, there are two circumstances which make Chinese much more strongly a member of the Japanese system of language varieties than either Ainu or Korean. One of the circumstances relates to the historical role China and Chinese played in

Japan. The other connects with the political and economic power of present-day China.

Throughout its long history Japan was strongly influenced by China. All advanced cultural forms before Meiji came to Japan from China, or at least through Chinese mediation. One of the most important influences was the Chinese language. Very much like Latin in Europe, Chinese performed in Japan the role of the official state language and the language of ideology. Before the Japanese syllabic script called *kana* developed, all documents were written in Classical Chinese. Even later, it remained the most prestigous written language variety in Japan. Even in 1866, a submission to the shogun, such as Maejima's famous proposal to abandon the use of characters, was of course written in Classical Chinese. Even today Classical Chinese survives as the language of Buddhist texts used in religious ceremonies, historical documents, and texts copied by Japanese calligraphers; to compose poetry in the language is a high-brow hobby. Classical Chinese, called *kanbun,* is taught in Japanese schools in the same way as Latin is still taught in some high schools in Europe and other Western countries.

The historical relationship as well as the current economic and political importance of China in East Asia have also recently led to an increased interest in the study of contemporary Standard Chinese in Japan.

Chinese is definitely not of the same parentage as Japanese and the grammatical structure of the language, both classical and modern, is completely different from the structure of Japanese. However, the Japanese writing system was borrowed from Chinese and the fact is still fully noticeable. Until the postwar reforms which simplified the shapes of the characters, the shapes remained exactly the same. The meanings changed to some extent but they, too, remain recognizable. Of course the pronunciation of the characters diverged drastically, both because in Japan it was impossible to retain the same variety of sounds as in Chinese, and because of the time that has elapsed since the readings were borrowed into Japanese.

From these facts it will be understandable that spoken Chinese is completely incomprehensible to a Japanese, and vice versa. However, simple titles of books, articles, etc., unless they contain unusual abbreviated characters, are mutually intelligible when sighted. When the Japanese face a whole text in Chinese, they can often guess at the overall meaning; this is because many characters still retain the same shape and have the same meaning, but also because the Japanese studied one variety of Chinese (Classical Chinese) at school. To learn to read contemporary Chinese texts is relatively simple for native speakers of Japanese. On the other hand, a Chinese finds it more difficult to handle Japanese texts. He does not understand the *kana* symbols used in Japanese between characters to mark grammatical relations, and the word order will not help him, because it is totally different in Japanese and Chinese. Also, until the quite recent boom in learning Japanese, very few people have ever studied the language in China.

English in Japan

Whatever we may think of the competence of the Japanese in English conversation, it is a fact that English is an important variety within the Japanese variety system. English is in fact (though not in law) a compulsory subject for all junior and senior high-school children in Japan. At school, it contributes toward a reading fluency in the roman script and provides an important practice in translating texts. It gives the community the knowledge of quite a number of English words, and supports the opportunity to borrow more and more. This opportunity is fully exploited: the Japanese language of today is full of international terminology borrowed through English, for example, *demokurashī* "democracy," *baraeti* "variety," and purely English words such a *kusshon* "cushion" or *kāsoru* "cursor." For many terms there is both an English borrowing and a domestic Japanese word (for instance, the more common word for "democracy" is *minshushugi*).

Of course, this position of English "within Japanese" does not imply that the Japanese are fluent speakers of English. The fact is that very few are. However, their reading competence is better, and on the whole the need for translations is catered for in Japan in a very satisfactory way.

A visitor to Japan soon finds that English is not spoken widely except in international hotels, luxury restaurants, and other tourist establishments in the largest cities. An English shop sign, even if unaccompanied by a Japanese one, does not guarantee that English will be understood. Often the use of English words on products manufactured in Japan for domestic consumption has a purely decorative function. The words are there to suggest the international class of the goods, not to be read.

The teaching of English in Japan is an extremely extensive business. Apart from high schools and universities there is a large number of private "conversation" schools, and the variety and amount of teaching materials produced and sold is amazingly large. The variety of English taught in Japan today is normally American English, though some British English, formerly dominant, still survives. However, when foreign names are transcribed into *katakana* (the more square of the two Japanese syllabic scripts), the transcription is based on British, not American pronunciation. The former American presidents Johnson and Carter are referred to as *Jonson* (not *Janson*) and *Kātā* (not *Karutoru*).

How English Changes

The adaptation of foreign names and other foreign words used in Japanese sentences is quite important. Foreigners who speak otherwise excellent Japanese are often misunderstood when they employ English words, without changing their pronunciation as is usual in Japanese. Rosewall, for instance, should be pronounced as *Rōzuōru,* Lloyd as *Roido,* McEnroe as *Makkenrō.* These adaptations follow quite definite rules that are not difficult to learn. All foreigners who are embarking on the study of Japanese should start by finding out how to pronounce correctly in Japanese their own names, the name of their country, their home town, and any other English words they are likely to frequently use. Note, by the way, that the pronunciation of foreign names and foreign words is adapted in all languages of the world. Imagine how surprised you would be if your neighbor came back from a trip to France and told you that he went to see an opera in Paris, pronouncing "opéra" and "Paris" in French!

English, when spoken by the Japanese, has a number of specific features. The distinction between r and l, b and v, and th and s are often lost. "Beer" and "veal," and "thick" and "sick" are often pronounced the same. The vowels of "pass," "map," and "cup," distinct in British English, become identical. The sentence usually has a flat intonation, and it may be difficult to judge which words are emphasized and which are not. In some cases it is difficult for Japanese speakers to make a distinction between the singular and the plural, or the present and the past tense. Of course, this is a purely grammatical problem, and there should be no doubt that the Japanese possess, as anyone else, the ability to distinguish between one object or two, or between what is happening at the moment and what happened in the past. Also, since there is no article in Japanese, it is not easy for the Japanese to decide whether they should say and write "home," "a home," or "the home." This problem they share with speakers of many other languages which do not have the distinction. Also, pronouns cause problems for many speakers. "He" and "she" are sometimes confused and used about people who are present. In most varieties of English to say "she told me" about a female speaker who is listening is considered to be rude.

Competence in English

It is intriguing that the Japanese have so far been some of the least proficient speakers of foreign languages in the world. Of course, we should not compare their competence with the competence in English of the Chinese from Hong Kong, Indians from India, or the Ghanians and some other African nationals. Even if the teaching of English is widespread, the language is a foreign, not a second language for them. All their education has been in Japanese, not in English.

Some other explanations have been given for the unusual situation. One is, of course, the fact that for average citizens there is so little need or opportunity to use English. The country is a large and independent cultural unit. Any foreign book of any importance is immediately translated into Japanese. Unlike in many smaller European countries or in the societies of the Third World, the average Japanese citizen has little need to read, and still less need to speak, a foreign language.

Another factor is the ancient methods of the teaching of foreign languages, which concentrate on grammar and translation and do not support the development of active competence. Moreover, English is used for grading students at entrance examinations. This means that most students have to abandon any thought of acquiring real competence in English: they must study hard to pass the examinations, and one cannot pass the exam because one knows English. "Examination English" is what is necessary.

Perhaps the most important factor is, however, the great distance between Japanese and the other major languages of the world. Not only is the structure of the language completely different from the structure of languages such as English, French, or German. The lexicon is also largely of a quite different stock. In addition, the system of communicative competence is vastly different from the system of the European languages. Of course, there are some differences between individual European languages and systems of communication. However, seen from the point of view of Japanese, they all are the same. The large number of borrowings notwithstanding, Japanese is still very different.

Speaking with Foreigners: Japanese or English?

Even if the English competence of a Japanese speaker may be rather low, in contact situations English is often selected in preference to Japanese. This can occur even when the foreign speaker's Japanese is better than the Japanese speaker's English. Many foreigners complain about this phenomenon. One asks a question in (reasonably fluent) Japanese but the reply comes back in (broken) English.

It is sure that we cannot simply accuse the Japanese of refusing to speak Japanese because they want to practice English. That may happen from time to time, but it is not the heart of the problem. The selection of a particular variety of speech for communication is mostly an unconscious process and the participants concerned do not necessarily understand themselves why they behave in the way they do. In the case of communities that are used to employing more than one language there are usually well established, mostly unconscious rules governing how to select a particular variety of language. For instance, one of my own rules is that the senior participant is granted the right of selection. However, this rule does not seem to be widely used by the Japanese. On the other hand, there seems to be a rule that the senior's language is the one which will be employed irrespective of what language he himself would like to use. Since in many cases foreigners are treated as seniors, this might account at least partly for the automatic selection of English by Japanese participants. Many people do feel that they should make communication for the foreigner easier. It must be admitted that the competence of the foreign speaker sometimes is really low and we should not be surprised if the Japanese want to help. It should be noted that in my own experience Japanese is normally selected in the case of participants who are known as semi-native speakers, and if the fact is not known at the beginning of a conversation, a switch is effected as soon as the fact becomes known.

Of course, established practices play an important role. If I may attempt a gross generalization, it seems to me that in communication between Japanese speakers and foreign students and staff at American universities English is more often selected than at similar Australian institutions. The established rule at my university seems to be that Japanese is spoken when all participants can speak Japanese and when one of them is a native speaker of the language. Surely, the Japanese speakers could complain that they are deprived of the right to practice English.

Let me add that English is of course not the only foreign language studied in Japan. French, German, and Russian occupy an important place both at the college (university) level of education and in the community at large. Other languages can be studied at specialized "foreign studies" universities and institutions of adult education. There are specialists for almost any language of importance, and even if they may not be very proficient in conversation, their reading competence is often amazingly high.

SETTING RULES:
AT WHAT TIMES AND PLACES
WE COMMUNICATE

"Setting rules" regulate the use of time and place of communication. It was mentioned above that we do not simply communicate whatever comes to our mind. Similarly, if we decide to communicate, this does not imply that we communicate immediately, and at any place we happen to be at the moment. Everyone probably has experienced pondering over "when should I tell her?" or "is this the proper place to say it?" The decision, the application of the setting rules, is not necessarily easy.

Visiting a Japanese Home

Suppose that you are visiting Mr. Takata's house in one of the suburbs of Kyoto. You said you would be coming at 3 P.M. and the first problem you have is that you are running late. To what extent is the time binding? Can you be late? The general answer to this question is positive. Unless the person with whom you have an appointment has other duties to perform immediately after your appointment, a precise time of arrival is not so important. To be late does not necessarily communicate much about the personality of the guest or his or her intention to be polite or impolite. Not only that people arrive late, some also arrive early. Of course, one can say on the whole that in the case of senior hosts people try to be more punctual or a little early. However, if your Japanese guest comes one hour late, it does not automatically follow that he intended to snub you. There may be a number of other circumstances at play. Anyway, you arrive at Mr. Takata's house ten minutes late. Nobody felt hurt.

When you ring the bell, a middle-aged woman who might be Mr. Takata's wife opens the door and invites you inside the entrance hall. You bow to each other, but contrary to your expectation there is no elaborate exchange of greetings or introductions. She may mention that it must have been difficult to find the house, or make a routine remark about bad weather, but obviously does not wish to be drawn into any more substantial polite exchange. You take off your shoes and your coat, prepared to proceed further into the house. However, there is a problem here. The right time to take off your hat, coat, and shawl was outside the house, before you rang the bell. Yet, since you are a foreigner, nobody will really take this failure of etiquette as intentional and communicative.

The correct place to engage in the greeting ceremony and to be introduduced is after you reach the lounge. Sometimes simple greetings are actually exchanged at the entrance, but even in that case the greeting ceremony in the lounge will usually not be omitted. However, it should be noted here that the rule is subject to social and perhaps also regional variation.

At the very beginning of what I have called the greeting ceremony you normally refer to your previous meeting with Mr. Takata, and it is obligatory to thank him again if he granted you on that occasion some favor—for instance invited you to a meal, helped you with your work, or something similar. The ceremony then continues, for instance, with comments on the weather, your recent circumstances, etc. Immediately at the conclusion of the greetings you hand over the present you brought for Mr. Takata and his family.

There are, of course many other rules of etiquette which you need to make this visit really successful, but the aim of this text is not to provide a full account of all possible behavior when visiting a Japanese family. The particular objective of this section is to emphasize that there are certain times and places when to perform particular communicative acts. If you forget to take your coat off before you enter the house, people will just smile, if they notice at all. However, if you forget to provide for an exchange of greetings at the time when such exchange is expected a general feeling of disappointment may result, and may be difficult to remove. If you forget to thank Mr. Takata for favors from your previous meeting at the beginning of the greeting ceremony, the failure will probably be noted. (As we shall mention later, there are simple routine expressions in Japanese to convey these thanks, but it is more difficult to do the same thing if the language in which you communicate is English.) There may be no other opportunity to hand over your present if you forget to do it before you sit down. Everything has its time and place. This is also fully true in the case of communication acts.

Appointments

The system of appointments to which we are so much used in Europe, Australia, or America means nothing else than that we draw a schedule of times and places for our communicative encounters. This schedule is usually strictly binding: a prior appointment is a reason for not accepting other invitations, and cancellations are exceptional.

It is not difficult to imagine that much of Japanese business and administration works on the same principle of appointments as we do. Industry and the political and administrative establishment of a modern society could not function otherwise. Perhaps in Japan the binding of an appointment may be less strict than we might expect and the schedule may more easily be changed. Yet, the difference is not great. One can behave pretty much in the same way as far as the timing of "business" appointments is concerned.

On the other hand, in the non-corporate (individual) sphere of communication, the temporal and spatial map for communication tends to be drawn in much less detail and is characterized by considerable fluidity. I have already given an example of appointments for visits to private homes. The same principle works throughout the society. Of course, this fact is not mentioned here as an encouragement to be late: but it may help to explain the behavior of other participants in contact situations. Perhaps we could even speak of a certain disinclination in the individual's sector to strictly schedule in advance times and place for communicative encounters. One important fact foreigners from those countries in which minutes count should remember is that to set private appointments in intervals of less than fifteen minutes is quite unusual in Japan. Unless there is a special reason, a statement such as "I'll be waiting there at five past ten" can evoke an outburst of laughter. It must be a joke. Moreover, it was already noted above that people do sometimes prefer not to set any time at all, and to leave the question of what to do next, for instance whether to go and eat together, a decision of the moment.

What Places are Suitable for Communication?

Because the standard of housing is still relatively low, because people often live very far away, and because space is frequently limited in offices as well, it is not easy to meet to talk at private homes or in people's offices. The existence of the large number of eating establishments and particularly of the enormous number of coffee shops and bars in any Japanese city can be explained not merely by particular entertainment patterns but also as a means of providing communication settings. When you meet a friend in town, the usual conclusion will be the Japanese phrase, *Ocha demo nomimashō ka?* "Shall we have a cup of tea?" The word "tea" here is a mere linguistic routine. Most people will have coffee. Care is given, where possible, to the selection of the establishment. If you are the guest you may not notice, but your host may mention directly that this is a good place, or it may become clear to you from indirect clues that this is not the first time he has been there.

Business will of course frequently be discussed in your contact's company area (there are meeting rooms and meeting spaces), but in the case of smaller companies that feel they cannot provide adequate space, you may be taken out to a coffee shop at which the company often has an account.

Since many readers of this book will frequently meet Japanese university teachers, it is not out of place to add a note on communicative settings important in the case of this professional group.

An Australian professor's secretary is trying to get in touch with her boss who is visiting Professor Goto in Tokyo. Her boss gave her Professor Goto's office as well as home number to be used in the case of emergency. The secretary rings and rings the office number—in the early morning, before lunch, several times in the afternoon, and stays to try again at 6:00 Tokyo time. No success. Is the number wrong?

The matter is more simple. Japanese academics do not usually have secretaries, and many come to their office only immediately before and after a class or a meeting. Many of them also teach at another college or institution, where they cannot be reached either. The correct way to contact them is by telephone early in the morning, but more safely in the evening, at their home. My students in Australia never call me at home, in particular not after office hours. However, when they study in Tokyo they must overcome their sense of distinguishing between office times and places and private settings and learn how to adjust to the Japanese norms. If they go on, attempting not to disturb their Japanese thesis supervisors at home, and calling their office numbers during the day, they may be unable to meet them at all. By the way, correspondence is usually also addressed to the home address rather than to the professor's office. This is both quicker and safer.

PARTICIPANT RULES: WHAT KINDS OF PARTICIPANTS COMMUNICATE

Occasionally we communicate with ourselves. For instance, I can make an uncomplimentary remark about myself to myself when I do something wrong. Or, as mentioned above, we can keep a diary or take notes for our own future use. However, normally more than one person is necessary for communication to take place. Of course, the other person is not always present. We can talk to someone on the telephone, write a letter, or read a book written by someone we have never met. In all these cases the other participant nevertheless exists. The participant rules specify what types of participants there are and how they interact in communication networks.

Paying Respect to Seniors

In Chapter Two I spoke of "seniors" and "juniors" as one important distinction between participants. With regard to this distinction foreigners in contact situations show two diametrically opposite trends. One is to let themselves be attracted too much by the outward communication of the distinction and assume that the difference is much more important than it actually is. The other trend is to disregard the distinction and assume that the relationship between people is the same as in the observer's own society. Either of these two extreme attitudes is incorrect. Distinctions of seniority do exist and even if not as dominant as the stereotypical images of Japan suggest, they do play an important role in communication.

A good game to play, if you can understand Japanese, is to watch middle-aged men on Tokyo trains after 10 P.M. There are many groups or pairs of businessmen who, after having entertained company guests, are returning home to their families. Watch the little distinctions in their speech and behavior. Guess what their relationship is at work, who is older, who is younger, who occupies a higher position, and all those other features that are obvious from the way they speak and behave. Even if you do not understand Japanese, you often can guess on the basis of their non-verbal behavior.

In many cases you will be able to make a correct judgment and mark one of the people as a clear senior. In other cases your conclusion will be that they are friends (equal in age and position). You will see older people who do not look like friends but seem to treat each other with equal respect. Sometimes you will recognize a subordinate who is older than the boss. However, until you become very good at the game, it will be difficult for you to make reliable judgments. If you travel with native speakers of Japanese compare your observations with theirs. You will be surprised how much they can guess about the identity and relationship between the observed people just on the basis of their patterns of communication.

Paying respect to a senior speaker within an encounter implies in Japan a large number of rules. The forms of address are more polite and may include the use of titles. Honorifics are employed. Non-verbal forms of behavior, such as posture, facial expression, bowing, and many others will vary. The topic of conversation is selected more carefully. Careful consideration is given to the needs and expectations of the senior in every possible way.

Respect will invariably be paid, but as I noted in Chapter Two the communication of politeness does not necessarily reflect real power. The real power of the senior may be much weaker than we are likely to believe.

Foreigners and Japanese Hierarchies

Foreigners who do not live and work in Japan are normally exempted from considerations of seniority. If you are one of them, you should not worry about it. Treat everyone with respect and your behavior will always be evaluated in a positive way. Some young foreigners, such as business executives, do occasionally assume a too friendly attitude to senior Japanese contacts. Extreme informality may invite a negative evaluation.

To learn to distinguish between senior and junior participants is not merely an academic exercise: the observation game suggested above has much sense. If we want to intercommunicate with the Japanese, we must know what is the mutual relationship between our partners and what it entails. When more than one Japanese take part in a contact encounter, you will be expected not to give precedence to a junior participant over a senior. However, if you watch correctly, you will find that the Japanese will often anticipate your problem and will indirectly indicate who should be greeted first and given the maximum of communicative attention.

The matter is more complicated with those foreigners who participate in Japanese networks in an intensive way. Here the issue is quite delicate. High-school students on exchange programs, foreigners who work in Japanese companies, other foreign residents who have benefited from the help of Japanese seniors, all these people will be expected, to some extent, to acknowledge the existence of the relationship of seniority in their communication in a quite active way.

In-group and Out-group Relationship

Another major division mentioned above is the division between "in-group" and "out-group" participants. This distinction is of course much more strongly communicated in other societies than the distinction between seniors and juniors and is therefore more familiar to us. Members of the in-group include the family, friends, people who work together, people who belong to relatively closed associations, and people who were closely associated before (such as former classmates) and retain a feeling of proximity.

In Japan in-group and out-group communication is very different. In-group communication requires the minimum of honorifics and is informal. Failure to adhere within an in-group to cultural or communication rules is noted less strongly than in out-groups. It is, for instance, possible to criticize openly other than senior members of your in-group networks. On the other hand, out-group communication requires various degrees of honorific speech and more formality in general; criticism in out-group networks is usually a much more serious matter.

Note that the distinction between senior/junior participants and in-group/out-group participants cross each other. In-groups include both seniors (e.g., parents, teachers, superiors) and juniors. Out-groups also consist of seniors (people who would be our seniors if they belonged to our in-group) and juniors (e.g., shop attendants, taxi drivers, etc.).

When one communicates with out-group senior participants who deserve special attention, in-group members can be temporarily given less attention. For instance, the presence of one's wife or children may be ignored when talking to a highly situated guest. This is not necessarily rude. In front of out-group seniors the Japanese show little respect to in-group seniors. In the case of telephone enquiries, company employees are instructed to refer to their boss as if the boss were a person of low status: the intention here is to emphasize that the out-group person is more important than even the head of one's institution.

Foreigners and Japanese In-groups

Real foreigners who are nevertheless closely associated with a Japanese network are not necessarily clearly classified as out-group; however, they rarely become full in-group members either. The best way they can approximate the status of an in-group member is through an introduction by a person who is highly respected in the network. This may be achieved by a letter of introduction, but recently the telephone is normally used for the purpose.

When approaching a Japanese speaker it is important to know of what in-groups he is a member. The three most important dimensions are the place of employment (company, university, etc.), the place of origin (in particular if regional), and the university or institution from which the person graduated. This knowledge will help you to build a bridge through common experience and acquaintances. Japanese speakers invariably remember this information and use it when they want to increase the degree of intimacy.

Foreigners who live in Japanese society (not those who merely physically live in Japan) are normally accepted in a number of in-groups. They are much less foreigners for such in-groups then they are in the society at large.

The classification of participants as senior/junior and in-group/outgroup may appear very exotic and unusual. However, we should clearly realize that the same phenomenon occurs in virtually every other society. Any civilized society defers to citizens senior by age. Also, we pay respect to distinguished citizens, as well as to our job superiors. The degree to which we communicate respect to seniors may differ, but it is never completely absent. In Japanese the degree is strong. Whether this means that the society is much more hierarchically organized is questionable. The in-group/out-group relationship, too, clearly survives in all contemporary societies.

Again, the degree of communicating about the relationship may differ, but basically, the same phenomenon is there. Sweeping statements about Japan as a society based on hierarchical principles, totally different from those of the societies of the West, are exaggerated and do not help our understanding of what actually happens when we communicate.

The Use of Address Terms and Names

The way people address each other is closely connected with their positions in communicative networks. Seniors are addressed differently from juniors, and in-group members from out-group persons. The same is true about the ways in which speakers refer to themselves.

In purely Japanese situations, where, of course, Japanese is used, parents and some senior relatives refer to themselves with kinship terms. For instance, a father speaking to his son does not normally say "I" but *otōsan*, or *papa*, "your father." Family seniors are not addressed with the pronoun "you" but again with a kinship term. So "Will you go?" is *Otōsan iku?* "Will father go?" not *Anata iku?* (*Anata* is one of the second-person pronouns.)

In the society at large people who have titles are addressed with the title (alone, or attached to their name), for instance Yoshida *shachō*, "Mr. (Company) President Yoshida," or Kida *sensei* "Mrs. Kida (a teacher)." These expressions are used instead of second person pronouns, for instance "Will Yoshida *shachō* go?" instead of "Will you go?" Note in particular that it is obligatory to use the title *sensei* for all teachers and doctors. To address them with a pronoun is unthinkable, and to address them with name followed by the suffix -*san* ("Mr./Mrs./Ms./Miss") is impolite. In most other cases, the name with -*san* (or the more intimate -*kun* or -*chan* in some instances) is preferred to any of the several second-person pronouns that exist in Japanese. Do not believe some textbooks that tell you that *anata*(you) is the polite second-person pronoun. It can be used among friends (mainly female) and to some junior addressees but never to a senior person.

The fact that second-person pronouns are used in contact situations conducted in foreign languages never concerns native speakers of Japanese. However, what may cause a problem are names. I have just said that in Japanese names are used frequently instead of second-person pronouns. However, these are normally family names, not first names. Consider the following situation. Mr. Kimura arrives in New York and the wife of his young neighbor in the suburb where they live asks what she should call him, what his first name is. His first name is Takeshi, but in Japanese only his father would call him Takeshi. His mother and sisters call him Takeshi-*san* (something like "Master Takeshi") and his school friends call him Kimura, or Kimura-*kun* (a few particularly close friends actually call him Takeshi-*kun*). The decision to let the young woman next door call him Takeshi is not a light one. The first name in Japan is only used within in-groups, never to seniors, and even in the case of its use to juniors the "hard" character of such address is softened by adding various suffixes.

Of course, many Japanese are familiar with American and other speech practices. Some of them do not mind disclosing their first names and are quite happy to be addressed in that way. Occasionally, however, you may encounter someone who is not used to the informal form of address, and if this is the case it may be better not to push too hard for the use of first names. However, some Japanese have found a way of escape: they ask people to call them by an English-sounding name which resembles their Japanese given name but is not identical with it. For instance, Michio says call me Michael. In this case the dilemma can be avoided: they are called by a first name, but not really their own.

Foreigners who are learning Japanese in Japan frequently ask people to call them by their first name, and many Japanese readily oblige. Some teachers of Japanese feel however that this is inappropriate. In Japanese schools not only older students but even first-grade primary school children are addressed with their surname (followed by -*san* or -*kun*). This is the usual Japanese pattern, and it does not imply any special degree of distance between the teachers and the pupil. It is necesary that foreign students in Japan realize that this is the case.

Acceptance of Foreigners in Japanese Networks

There are many views about the relative ease with which foreigners can penetrate into Japanese networks. Broadly speaking there are three camps: those who maintain that the Japanese are "most friendly and easy to talk to," those who bitterly complain, and those who perhaps could be called the realists.

Many foreigners who visit Japan for a short period of time and have had previous contacts there, usually belong to the first category. They are passed from hand to hand, and are looked after, fed, and treated with great respect. The Japanese ask a lot of questions, freely talk about their own problems, and are very friendly. One of the necessary conditions for being put in this category is good contacts. Your contacts will not necessarily be people you have met yourself, they can be friends of friends, to whom you have been properly introduced. When you go to Japan, arrange for recommendations and you will see that they do wonders.

The second group are those who complain. It is a curious fact, reported by many observers, that the longer you stay in Japan, the more you study the language, and the more you become used to the country, the less you may be accepted into Japanese networks. The reason is that the less "foreign" you are, the more likely it is that the normal Japanese rules for evaluating behavior and accepting new members into networks will be applied. And it is not always easy for the Japanese themselves to be accepted into new groups.

A few years ago I participated in an international meeting at which the relationship between foreigners and the Japanese was discussed. Many academics who had lived in Japan over an extended period of time were present and a little spark switched on a chain reaction in which almost everyone poured out his heart. Stories were told of attempts to become friends with the Japanese, attempts which ended up in a complete failure. It was claimed that the Japanese refused to speak Japanese, did not accept invitations, and sometimes cooled off in a relationship that could have been considered as virtually permanent.

I had no doubt that many of the stories were perfectly true or only slightly exaggerated. The same thing of course happens everywhere in the world. It is not easy to get accepted into established networks, and the Japanese who live in Australia, Britain, or America complain in the same way. There are few "vacancies" in existing networks, and when they occur, they are filled with people who give promise to be the best members. Foreigners naturally miss out in competition with native "applicants."

I happened to know some of the people at the meeting. Their Japanese was improving but it was not really sufficient to communicate about everything. Japanese friends, as friends everywhere, discuss occasionally quite interesting and linguistically somewhat difficult topics, and someone who can barely manage social small talk is a nuisance when anything more complicated than everyday life is discussed. Moreover, some of these people were obviously unprepared to yield an inch of what they considered "correct" behavior, but what actually was nothing else than conventions of the society into which they were born. They were people who insist on helping ladies into their coats, joke on all occasions, laugh too loudly, sit in a too relaxed way, and try to converse with shop assistants, . . . With regard to communication and cultural rules, they did not change at all after coming to Japan.

The most surprising thing was that they seemed to believe that being such nice and friendly people in their own manner gave them the *right* to be accepted as members in any Japanese network they wanted to join. But no such right exists.

The third group of foreigners are people who have grown out of both the "first love" stage and the stage of "complaints." They understand that to establish friendship networks in Japan is like making friends everywhere else. Difficult. But it pays off.

How to Make Friends

The following comments on making friends in Japan, though useful primarily for young people who come to Japan to study Japanese, should also be of some interest to other categories of foreigners. First, they should understand that the most important factors in the establishment of a friendship network are psychological closeness, the need for associates on both sides, and communicative compatibility. If we want to make friends, we must satisfy the first requirement by learning more about the daily life, thought, and sensitivities of the Japanese, and try to adjust. Some basic comments on all these points were offered in Chapter Two of this book. In order to satisfy the second condition, we should have something to offer. This will often be the opportunity of practice in a foreign language, normally English. Do not become nervous if a Japanese wants to practice English with you. There is so little opportunity to do that in

Japan, and if you are in the country you yourself will have plenty of opportunity to speak Japanese on other occasions! Of course, it is important to be careful not to be used just simply for conversation practice, but you will be able to judge for yourself in what direction the relationship is developing. Experience shows that if it is toward friendship, Japanese is likely to automatically replace English as the language of your communication.

Apart from the psychological and sociological factors, the techniques of communication can contribute to the establishment and maintenance of friendship to a considerable extent. Some such techniques are universal, others are more specifically Japanese. First, if you wish to enter into a friendship relationship, try to build a firm bridge between yourself and your Japanese partner. This can be achieved by finding out the maximum number of common friends and acquaintances and shared experiences, and by repeatedly raising them as topics in conversation. The fact that your potential friend, or his or her family or friends, knows your teacher, has been to your country, or has a similar hobby, helps tremendously in the first stages of the developing of a relationship. In friendship networks everywhere, common friends and shared interests are among the most typical topics discussed.

Secondly, do not hesitate to talk about yourself and ask questions about your partner. This again is what friends do. Of course, while doing so, you must realize that the way you ''present yourself'' in conversation is subject to different constraints in different systems of communication. For example, in Japanese you are not expected to show off as much as you might be allowed in the USA. We shall return to this issue when discussing the content rules.

Thirdly, try to adapt your communicative behavior to the norms of the Japanese system. This will make you less conspicuous and spare your Japanese friends much embarrassment. No one is eager to walk around with people who communicate deviance whenever they move, whatever they do, and as soon as they utter a single word. It is necessary to be dressed as expected, to avoid strong means of non-verbal behavior (body movements, gestures, laughter, etc.), and in general to communicate in a way in which a Japanese friend would communicate. If you are not sure, the correct thing is to ask.

Also, if the language used is Japanese, you should accept that a fair amount of competence, including reading competence, will be needed. Even casual conversation refers to what was in the morning paper, this week's magazines, to the current best-sellers. It is also necessary to pay proper attention to honorifics. You should achieve the ability to employ the plain ("informal") style of honorifics, which is used in friendship networks, and apply it as appropriate, without losing at the same time the ability to speak in the polite ("formal") style. If you are too informal, the relationship will suffer, but if you are too formal you will never be able to reach a high degree of intimacy.

Finally, it is necessary to accept that your Japanese friends will have other friends. Of course, occasionally one can meet Japanese who have not developed wide friendship networks, or someone who would like to "keep the foreigner for himself." However, such cases will be limited. The most usual form is friendship with people who have already established other ties. Do not try, as some foreigners do, to separate your partner from his or her existing networks. Rather than that, try to join in yourself and participate in the activities of the group network. Of course, the group may have already established rules which must be honored. For instance, there may be seniors and juniors. This is common in particular in some sports clubs in which there are *senpai* (seniors) and *kōhai* (juniors). Initially, your membership may be marginal and you may not be expected to speak up too much, but your status will probably change in time as you gain full membership.

Parties

In Chapter Two a number of types of Japanese parties was mentioned. Although informal "standing" parties, where people move freely, select partners, and talk to everyone they wish are becoming quite common, many parties are using seating arrangements, either in a room furnished with tables and chairs, or on tatami. In these networks refreshments or meals are usually served. There may be a guest of honor, who is then the real guest of honor, not merely an excuse for getting together: the fact that the party is being held to honor him or her, or them (if there is more than one) is communicated clearly and repeatedly. It is quite common for foreigners to become guests of honor. Parties of this type always have a chairperson, who distributes the right of speech. It is not necessary to mention that while someone speaks, all other participants remain silent and do not talk, even in a low voice, with their neighbors. Since parties of this type are very common among people of all social classes, many Japanese develop an excellent ability for public speaking. Foreigners should be prepared by assuming that they will be asked to contribute, too, in particular if they are the guests of honor or in a position close to that.

Many informal parties and gatherings at which not all participants know each other commence with "self-introduction" speeches. The tone and length is given by the first few speakers; sometimes to declare one's own name and affiliation will suffice, sometimes more information about work, interest, or reason for presence are expected. Students of Japanese should gradually develop competence to deliver these "self-introduction" speeches fluently in the Japanese language.

The traditional party may be preceded, followed, or fully replaced by a modern "standing" party. On these occasions the large integrated network of the traditional party splits into smaller groups. It is quite common for "dyadic networks" (i.e., networks consisting of two participants only) to be formed. When a third person joins, one of the original two members can be excused and depart in order to create a new network. This is just the same behavior as at any American or Australian cocktail party.

However, often larger than dyadic networks are formed, especially if one of the participants is a senior. The senior person then becomes the "pivot" and even if he or she does not speak all the time, communication quite clearly develops around him or her. Pivot networks are not unusual in other speech communities but they may be less common than in Japanese. In contact situations they should be recognized and the necessity to acknowledge the existence of the pivot accepted: for instance, it is not polite to channel conversation in the group toward a topic which may not suit the pivot, to try to split the network, etc.

Another variety of entertainment network is a "pool network," in which there is no particular pivot and participants address the whole group rather than any particular individual. This network is especially common in informal friendship groups in informal settings, for instance during a lunch break or when a small group of friends is having coffee in a coffee shop. This network can of course split into dyadic networks, but often it doesn't. The group continues communicating as a group, in which everyone who wants to talk talks, and everyone who decides to remain silent can do so.

"Aizuchi" or "Back-channeling"

One rather important detail about the behavior of Japanese speakers in networks is the use of verbal and non-verbal signals to affirm that they are listening. Short words such as the English "yes," "right," "hm," (*hai, ē, sō desu ne, naruhodo,* etc.), or nodding appear after almost each phrase, sentence or group of sentences uttered by the other participant. The frequency is much higher than in English. It is impolite to imply, by dropping *aizuchi,* that you are not de facto listening.

The use of *aizuchi* transfers easily to contact situations in which English is spoken, and Japanese participants who are not used to English speakers will normally be worried if the back-channel signals are not used by other participants as frequently as they would be in Japanese. Foreigners who live in Japan often acquire the habit of back-channeling and use the device even in their own language.

Public Networks

I shall use the expression "public network" to refer to encounters of participants who are not known to each other and intercommunicate in public settings such as the street, means of transport, or shops.

Since Japanese cities normally consist of a web of streets and little lanes, and since place names are not clearly marked, your Japanese friends will often draw for you a map of the locality which you are supposed to reach. Still, it will often be necessary to ask for directions. A minimum amount of Japanese is normally sufficient to do so, but if you do not speak Japanese and want to be sure, the best way is to ask a Japanese (for instance, a hotel receptionist) to write on a piece of paper where you want to go. You can then show it to anyone (including a taxi driver), and the system works marvellously well.

When you are leaving a railway station you may be tempted to ask the railway employee who is collecting used tickets for further directions, but you will find that he will normally be uncooperative. Quite understandably so, because he has a lot of work to do. However, in front of any larger railway station there is a police box (*kōban*) and one of the main functions of the police in Japan is to give directions. They usually have detailed and up-to-date maps of their area. If there is no police box, I usually buy a packet of chewing-gum at a tobacconist's and subsequently ask for the information I need. Shop attendants may be busy or they may have even less knowledge of the area than you do. Of course, you can stop anyone who looks like a local resident, and normally you will be given the information you need. The Japanese themselves use this method only as the last recourse, but foreigners are allowed to engage in a number of kinds of behavior that native speakers do not normally practice. I usually select in this case a middle-aged woman, rather than a man, and I do not ask children.

The Japanese who live overseas are used to consulting maps. However, new arrivals, when invited, will feel more secure if you draw a map for them which they can follow without having to ask.

Taxi drivers in Japan split into two groups: those who talk with customers and those who don't. If a taxi driver looks uncommunicative, do not try to draw him into a conversation. Only very few will have a smattering of English. Of course, occasionally you will find a taxi driver who will "speak English" and will be very happy to practice with you. By the way, the seat next to the driver is taken in Japan only if the back seats cannot take more customers. Do not try to sit next to the driver if you are the only customer, because he might feel not merely surprised by the unusual situation but also insecure. The custom of sitting in the back of the car is so strongly ingrained in the Japanese that they may make a mistake and even sit in the back seat when they are overseas and are being driven in a private car, with no other passenger in it. If this happens, it is not intended to communicate "I consider you to be my chauffeur." Also, passengers do not touch the door locks in Japanese taxis, as all doors are controlled by the driver. Hence, if your Japanese guest fails to open the door for you after you let him into your car, this should not be seen as a sign of communicating anything about his interpretation of the situation or as a message about his personality.

Shopping

In normal Japanese shops, except perhaps those which sell products at a discount, attendants do not exert pressure on shoppers to buy. You will also find that after the sale is decided on and the attendant disappears with both your money and the things you bought, she will definitely come back with the goods beautifully wrapped and with the exact change. It is not common to talk to attendants, particularly in large department stores, in a half-personal way exchanging, for instance, greetings about the weather, explaining circumstances of the purchase, and expressing or eliciting views. Not that this would never happen, but in some cases it can embarrass the attendant, especially if she or he is young. Conversely, Japanese partners can embarrass their overseas host when shopping together if they pay too little attention to the shop attendant, "treating him/her as a non-person." This may happen both through influence from the Japanese system and because of "simplification" of behavior due to losing control over communication rules as a result of using English.

Dealing with Japanese Officialdom Networks

Japanese public servants in many cases make up the elite that runs the country. Only the best graduates of the top universities can become the executive staff of the Ministry of Finance, the Ministry of International Trade and Industry, the Foreign Ministry, or the Ministry of Education. Some other jobs in the government service are not so difficult to obtain, but the consciousness of being a representative of the country, rather than a public *servant* is strong. This, understandably, influences communication in native situations. Public servants, especially of the older type, often assume the role of senior participants in encounters. They like to have their status confirmed by other participants (through communicative deference, apologies, etc.), but once this is done they do not always stick to the bureaucratic rules, and can show an amazing degree of flexibility. Of course, we must accept that there are long established general rules that cannot be bent under any circumstances.

The contact of foreigners with Japanese government employees is limited. Of course, one passes through immigration control and customs on arriving in the country. Some of my friends who speak Japanese tell me that they never speak the language to the immigration and customs officers at Narita, just in case the officer in charge happens to believe that something must be wrong with a foreigner who speaks Japanese. To go to the Immigration Office in Tokyo to have one's visa extended used not to be the most memorable experience. I hear that the situation has somewhat improved; here, one can perhaps argue that to visit the immigration office is far from being a cheerful occasion in many other countries as well.

Many foreigners are scared of going to the city office to register for obtaining the Alien Registration Certificate. Of course only those who stay for longer than a certain time limit are required to do so; they must carry the Registration Certificate even when they go shopping at their local supermarket. The situation at the city office, where foreigners register, is really taxing. On one side, foreigners are angry because they are fingerprinted "like common criminals." On the other side, Japanese employees are necessarily antagonized by the repeated experience of dealing with frustrated foreigners. However, most of those who, like myself, have been through these unpleasant encounters will agree that they are not representative of Japan. Once you leave the office, the sun shines again.

Japanese Companies Overseas

Some information on the working of Japanese companies has already been given in Chapter Two. Much more could be said, but only a few comments on communication in Japanese companies overseas will be added here.

In Chapter Two I emphasized the horizontal rather than the vertical character of decision making in many Japanese companies. The opinion of many people is taken into consideration, either formally or informally, and the final decision is not necessarily based on the attitude of the head of the organization. The question is to what extent non-Japanese executives can participate in this process.

At present, the structure of the executive body of most Japanese companies overseas consists of two layers. One is the more or less limited stratum of people who have been sent from Japan. Because of problems in obtaining long-term visas and partly because of company policies, these people are often short-term residents and return to Japan before they get the opportunity to become fully acquainted with the situation in the country concerned. The second stratum consists of local executives, who normally have no command of Japanese. As their service for the company extends, they come to identify with the company and feel frustrated when their voice is not adequately heard.

What does normally happen? Even though this may not be a company policy, the Japanese executives tend to form a somewhat separate network. For instance, they say "we speak English the whole day, so at least at lunch-time we want to relax in Japanese." However, the lunch situation is one of the occasions for informal dicussions, and since usually the non-Japanese executives cannot speak Japanese well enough to participate in these encounters, they become Japanese-only occasions. The foreign executives miss out not only on spoken communication networks. They cannot of course read either. Much information from the parent company comes in English, but the importance of information available only in Japanese is basic, and foreign employees of the company miss out here as well.

I cannot discuss here the question of whether or not Japanese companies intentionally try to keep the decision-making process in the hands of ethnically Japanese members of staff, recruited and trained at the parent company. Whatever the case may be today, much more integration of networks within companies will be necessary in the future and this cannot be achieved without much more effort at integrating both the formal and informal communication networks. Unless the Japanese employees can be expected to abandon the use of Japanese altogether, it will be necessary for more and more foreign executives to develop competence in the Japanese language. This is not impossible to achieve if graduates with basic competence in the language are recruited and provided with additional training in Japan.

CONTENT RULES:
WHAT IS COMMUNICATED

Transmission of content is the actual reason we communicate. Of course, the content we transmit can be of various types. One important type is factual information about reality (i.e., a description of what happened, how things are, etc.). Normally when we speak about information we mean this type of content. I shall call this type *factual*. However, the content of communication is more varied than this. People normally transmit various types of information about themselves, their social and other qualities, attitudes, intentions, etc. This type of information can be referred to as *presentational* content, because it relates to the ways individuals present themselves. We can also speak of additional types of content, such as *appellative*, when an appeal for information or performance of an act is transmitted. Almost all speech acts have a little of each, and much of one of these types of content. The process of communication of all these types of content is subject to different rules and strategies in different systems of communication. I shall try to outline some of the differences which exist between English and Japanese.

Good and Bad Topics

In Japanese there are few topics that would be unsuitable under normal circumstances. Of course, questions that might cause embarrassment will not be asked, and it can be said that the Japanese are normally very considerate speakers. Subject to this limitation, politics, religion, or personal matters can all be discussed. After some experience you will agree that the Japanese are frank and ready to not only communicate about neutral topics but also share quite personal information about themselves, their beliefs, and their attitudes.

One topic that was formerly constrained in the case of some middle-class speakers was money, and even today you will find people who do not wish to discuss the price of things, salaries, or any other financial matters. Many others will not mind and will initiate an extensive discussion that may even surprise a foreigner.

On the other hand, reference to some items, tabooed in English, is common in Japanese. For instance, the word *o-shiri*, "one's bottom," is not constrained. This can cause amusement among learners of the language. In my variety of communicative competence I am not allowed to say, as an excuse, "I am busy," and I am expected to refrain from communicating that I am busy through non-verbal behavior ("looking busy"). However, in Japanese, there are no constraints in this respect. A Japanese professor can easily say "I am busy" when sending a student away, without being rude.

Stewardesses on Japan Airlines flights sometimes look very busy. This communicates to the Japanese customers that they are properly looked after; some Western customers may take it for a sign of lack of experience.

Topics in Contact Situations

It is not unusual that simplification of content occurs in contact situations and as control over content is lost, questions that are not considerate or would not be asked otherwise can occur. For instance, someone may ask a female participant about her age, or raise a "childish" topic. This happens to non-Japanese participants as well.

In contact situations, so-called contact topics, mentioned already above, are always good. You can talk about common friends, familiar places, and common experiences. Asking questions about Japan, and comparing Japan with one's own country is also a good and safe topic for any occasion. This is useful to realize, because in some English-speaking networks, though not so much in the USA, these topics are not positively evaluated. The reason for this negative evaluation is that speakers are supposed to treat everyone as an individual, not as a representative of a social group. In these English-speaking networks, flat generalizations—for instance, statements about "the Japanese"—are avoided; the same is true with regard to expressions such as "in my country." By the way, the Japanese equivalent *waga kuni de wa* would be equally too emotional and overloaded. However, many Japanese speakers will show little hesitation to speak in contact situations as representatives of Japan, even if they actually do not feel like that. To present factual information about one's own country in a completely neutral and detached way is relatively difficult, and many Japanese participants may sound too "nationalistic."

Communicating about Oneself: Admitting Knowledge

Although in practice it is not uncommon to find people who speak about themselves a lot, the norm in Japanese, except in very informal situations, is the opposite: to speak about oneself as little as possible. In particular, to directly claim or admit knowledge or competence is not supposed to be in very good taste. However, some speakers of Japanese can manage admirably well to communicate that they actually knew what you told them, without explicitly saying that. In some English-speaking communities, to speak about your own competence is not constrained. Take, for example, an American academic who arrived in a Japanese department overseas and considered it natural to tell his new Japanese colleagues about all he and his wife knew of Japanese culture, and it was not little. The Japanese members of the department were shocked by what they considered to be an unbearable degree of exaggerated self-propagation. It took several months before they discovered that he was a genuinely competent and nice fellow.

It is quite common that foreign speakers of Japanese are complimented on their knowledge of the language, especially in the first stages of the learning process. To just stand and giggle, as some learners do, means that you are accepting the compliment as true, and this should never happen. Neither is the correct reply, *Sukoshi dake hanasemasu* "I can only speak a little," which is a strange sentence anyway. A direct denial is necessary, such as *Iie, mada zenzen. . .* "No, not really. . ." How to respond to compliments such as *O-jōzu desu ne* "[Your Japanese] is excellent" has now become an important component of introductory courses of Japanese.

The matter is not that in Japanese one would hide one's competence or never admit any knowledge. As in any other culture, modesty is sometimes an artificial device calculated at impressing others. Besides, when it matters, ways of communicating about one's knowledge are found. Direct communication can for instance occur in a job interview, but even in this case speakers are careful not to give the impression of self-propagation or boasting. However, normal communication about one's abilities is not direct or immediate; the suitable setting for disclosing one's competence is carefully considered and it may take quite some time before the information can be communicated. When it does not matter at all, for instance, in a casual once-only encounter, the fact that we know, too, or even better, can remain uncommunicated. The Japanese frequently transfer these rules to contact situations in which English is spoken, and their denial of knowledge or competence is taken for truth. It may not be at all.

Compliments addressed by foreigners to senior Japanese speakers can also be inappropriate. After a seminar given by a Japanese professor, junior foreign participants sometimes come and compliment his theories or delivery without realizing that if they express their judgment about the quality of the paper, they are actually putting themselves into a superior position. By evaluating they say "I know better." The correct behavior in this situation is just to bow and say "Thank you."

Likes and Desires

In in-group communication in the family or among friends, speaking about one's own likes and dislikes is unconstrained. However, in an even slightly more formal situation such reference is avoided, either because of consideration for other speakers' attitudes, or simply because to assert one's own position or communicate a negative evaluation is itself negatively evaluated.

The reluctance to express one's preferences and desires is also reflected in the use of the grammatical form called the desiderative. Many Japanese textbooks introduce at an early stage these forms which mean "I want to. . .", "do you want to. . .", etc. However, for a beginner, these forms are very difficult to use. To assert one's wish to do something is often (though not, of course, always) inappropriate. To refer to someone else's wishes is still worse. Some students believe that if they say *Kyō kaimono ni ikitai desu ka*, using the desiderative form *ikitai* of the verb *iku* (to go), they are saying "Would you like to go shopping today?" However, the Japanese desiderative does not perform the function of turning sentences into more polite sentences as the English phrase "would you like to. . ." does. The best way to say "Would you like to go shopping today?" is to simply say "Will you go shopping today?" using the basic (present/future) form of an honorific form of the verb "to go" *(irasshaimasu ka)*. But not the desiderative.

Yes or No: Expressions of Agreement and Consent

The fact that the Japanese hesitate to say "no" is well known, and often exaggerated. First, it is not only the Japanese who do it.

Everyone hesitates to create a situation of disagreement unless it is really necessary. This is particularly true if the other participant is a highly respected senior. For instance, to say in a discussion, "No, I disagree" may be a very strong statement and most cultivated native speakers of English will handle the situation in a more elegant way. Secondly, a straight "no" does exist in Japanese when less sophisticated superiors respond to inferiors. Here English, on occasions, may be more indirect than Japanese. Thirdly, speakers very often remain undecided, both in English or in Japanese, and in such cases we should not be surprised that participants in the encounter will be unable to say whether the answer was "yes" or "no." Fourthly, a clear disagreement or refusal is often communicated even to senior participants. Even though this happens by means other than simply saying "no," the fact that disagreement or refusal were communicated will be obvious to any native speaker of Japanese. For instance, the sentence *Sō desu ne, muzukashii desu ne* "Yes, well, it's difficult" will normally mean a refusal, and cannot be interpreted as a hesitation. The same is true about *Sumimasen* "I'm sorry," *Kangaete okimasu* or *Kōryo shimasu* "I'll consider it," or any other delaying strategy. Response by silence of course clearly means "No."

When foreigners are engaged in negotiations with representatives of Japanese organizations, they often prefer to ask an experienced Japanese friend to accompany them, and after the encounter is over, they check their interpretation of the negotiations with him. Although they themselves may have doubts, the Japanese participant normally doesn't. The attitudes of the person with whom the negotiations took place are mostly clear to him. Of course, as mentioned above, some points may have been left undecided or ambiguous, but this is what also happens in English and other languages and cannot be claimed as a unique feature of Japanese.

To conclude, we can say that the word "no" certainly is used less frequently in Japanese than in English. The way that disagreement or refusal are communicated is more indirect, but in most cases no ambiguity results.

One additional explanation for the relatively low frequency of the word *iie* (*ie*, *iya*, etc.) in Japanese in comparison with English "no" may be the fact that in English "no" is employed as the introductory component of polite refusal formulae in which the second part of the formula also contains an expression of negative attitude. For instance, we can say "No, I am afraid that. . ." or "No, I don't think that. . ." In Japanese these polite formulae would probably be best rendered by *Sō desu ne* "Well, that's right but. . ." or *Dō deshō ka* "How is [that]?" and these expresions do not include an introductory negative component. To start any negative response with *iie* is a bad habit of many foreign speakers of Japanese and it is worth paying attention to its removal.

The word *hai* is tricky. Normally it is translated as "yes," but it is actually a mere *aizuchi* ("back-channelling") devise and as such actually means something like "I understand what you say" or "I am listening." It does not necessarily mean "Yes, I agree" or "Yes, I will do it." Also, in some cases, answers to negative questions (e.g., "Isn't that strange") will use *hai* in the sense "it isn't," where "no" would be appropriate in English. It is better to check in these cases what the answer was. Such checks are not unusual even between native speakers and will not attract much attention

Perhaps this is the place to add a few words about the expression of displeasure in Japanese. Again, direct and strong communication of displeasure is less common than in English. You will of course see people who are obviously angry and who shout. However, when a foreign supervisor of Japanese employees in a Tokyo branch of an overseas organization shouts angrily at his subordinates, this can became a source of amusement rather than indignation. It is funny that he lost temper over an insignificant detail and could not control himself. Communication of displeasure in a more indirect way, for instance, by making a stern face and refusing to respond to the friendly attitude of the Japanese employees would have communicated his intention much more efficiently.

Humor and Joking

Humor is an important type of information, transmitted in communication acts, though not of course of what we called above "factual" information. We shall not stop here to consider what humor actually is. What is important is that it is a fact of communication (not simply "culture" in general, or language) and that it secondarily carries "presentational" meaning, that is, it communicates about the qualities and attitudes of speakers.

Those who maintain the one-sided picture of the gray, hard-working, and sinister Japan have missed the point that the Japanese system of communication contains a strong component of humor. Within the traditional culture, the Kyogen (medieval farces, often performed today) and the *rakugo* or *manzai* (humorous story telling) have been well preserved, occupy an important place, and are loved by the Japanese of all age groups. Many other genres of humor existed. Japan has always had both faces of a healthy culture, the serious and the laughing one.

Modern comedies and humorous sketches are of course well established on the stage as well as the film screen and as components of radio and television programs; although there may be no truly great author of humorous novels, humor as an accompanying element does enter into both classical and contemporary Japanese literature; weekly and other magazines devote much space to humor; and all Japanese newspapers publish daily cartoons, which for many people is the first part of the paper they see. Daily conversation in Japanese is full of jokes and wit. When you see people in the street or in a coffee shop talking and laughing, they are not laughing for nothing.

We must realize that "the language of humor" is not universal. Humor is often dependent on a particular language. Even if they may read and speak English quite well, people from the European continent or America may have problems in understanding why cartoons in the British press are funny. British comedies are not necessarily funny in America and vice versa. Even if we know Japanese quite well, we may miss the point of much of the Japanese humor. When I was studying in Japan in the 1960s I took a "course" in reading Machiko Hasegawa's cartoon series "Sazae-san," which was appearing in the most popular newspaper, *Asahi Shinbun*. With a friend I studied the cartoon daily. After the first month, I was able to read the cartoon independently, but I still had to go occasionally for an additional lesson, when I could not understand what was funny about a particular story. Sazae-san, by the way, is available in a series of books (there is even a television cartoon), and I can recommend it sincerely to anyone who intends to embark on the study of Japanese humor.

Not only that humor is not universal. There are also social constraints on some of its genres. In Japanese middle-class conversation, constant joking is not necessarily highly evaluated. Too many word puns are a ''lower social class'' way of speaking. A foreigner who makes a joke in each sentence he utters will be tolerated but his speech will not be as highly appreciated as he might think. The short humorous stories (jokes) that are so popular in some European countries do not belong to the original Japanese genres of humor, and although gaining more and more popularity, may often remain uncomprehended. Jokes with clear sexual overtones appear in the lowly weekly magazines and their presentation is likely to be connected with that context and evaluated negatively in middle-class conversation.

Are They Polite?

Students of verbal and non-verbal etiquette still do not agree on what it means to be polite. However, it seems that the acceptance of the existing distance between those communicating is the basic characteristic of politeness. By greeting someone, we acknowledge the fact that we know the person (i.e., we indicate our proximity to him/her); by being considerate in raising delicate topics, we acknowledge the right of other people for privacy (i.e., we respect their right to remain distant from us); by using a polite form of address, we may communicate our acceptance of the seniority of a person (i.e., we acknowledge greater distance in terms of status). In any case, to be polite means to communicate a particular type of content: politeness. Hence, there is no doubt that the consideration of politeness is a matter of content rules.

Of course, politeness is not necessarily communicated through language. We can communicate it by various non-verbal means. The Japanese bow comes immediately to mind. We can also be polite or impolite by being dressed in a particular way, and it is polite to give someone a gift. In the present section of this chapter, only some general strategies will be considered. Individual cases of the communication of politeness are treated in other sections.

Are the Japanese really as polite as the popular stereotype has it? As on many other previous occasions, the first hurdle is again the word ''the Japanese.'' You can meet people in Japan who are only polite when apologizing to a superior. On the other hand, there are others, in particular middle-aged and older women, who seem to live within one continuous ceremony of politeness. The second problem is who we compare then with. Some foreigners certainly do not stand on ceremony, but there are others who put much emphasis on politeness.

On the whole, one can perhaps generalize and say that the Japanese do communicate politeness frequently. There are many communicative acts or encounters that are primarily or to a large extent used to communicate politeness. The *aisatsu* (''greeting'') visit is an example: people go and pay a visit (either private or of a business nature) just as an expression of politeness. Apart from polite or contact topics, no ''business'' content is discussed. That is left for other occasions. The *aisatsu* visit can be used to initiate contact or to reassert that contact is still desirable, and that the recipient of the visit is considered the party of higher status. Also, seeing people off or welcoming them on arrival are situations of great importance in Japan. Traffic terminals of all kinds not only in Japan but throughout the world frequently display groups of Japanese travelers accompanied by a group of well-wishers: the whole encounter has no meaning except for communicating politeness. Ceremonies such as weddings or funerals are very well attended. The number of guests is sometimes amazing, and with the growing ''affluence'' in the society it seems to be rather increasing than decreasing. There will be no necessity to emphasize that for the invited participants such ceremonies have no practical aims whatsoever: both as a whole and in their individual components, they are exercises in politeness. Even encounters which are predominantly of a practical nature often start with extended *aisatsu* acts and close with another *aisatsu* scene. Presents, which are a means of communicating the interest in maintaining a close relationship, remain a pervasive custom practiced in almost any situation of social and business life. Perhaps the frequent occurrence of all this behavior, which is basically oriented toward the communication of politeness, is less characteristic for the young than for the older Japanese. However, it is necessary to realize that it is not restricted to the middle or upper class.

The channels of communication of politeness are equally varied. One way of expressing politeness is through the use of particular dress. In Japan, proper formal dress, mostly abandoned in the West, is used for weddings, funerals, and other ceremonial occasions. Objects (presents), another medium (channel) of transmitting politeness, are given/received or exchanged. The medium of "body language" is extensively used, both in the form of the Japanese bow and in constraints on standing, sitting, walking, eye contact, and other forms. The use of speech serves of course as a vehicle for politeness in many ways, being a means for the exercise of considerateness, selection of topics and verbal expressions, various types of greetings, and polite phrases, in which Japanese abounds. Finally, unlike in English, which has lost even the difference between the pronouns "thou" and "you," politeness is transmitted through the medium of linguistic forms called honorifics. More information on honorifics will be given in the next chapter.

The Universality of Politeness

All this may sound very discouraging. Is it possible for a foreigner to ever penetrate this wall of strange and exotic customs? Actually little if anything in this list is exotic. When we learn about foreign cultures we often forget that very similar "strange" customs exist in our culture as well and that it is only our familiarity with them that is responsible for the fact that they do not attract our attention. For instance, the idea of a courtesy visit is not quite unusual in any Western system of communication. When I travel, I sometimes make several per day. Certainly seeing people off when they travel a long distance is not unheard of. We do attend weddings, funerals, even christening parties, and some of the behavior on those occasions is strongly ceremonial and impossible to penetrate for people from other cultures (or even sub-cultures of our own culture). We often use social talk at the beginning of business encounters, and close a working meeting with a younger colleague by asking "And how is your mother?" Presents are exchanged, dress is discussed, and sometimes, quite importantly, we pay attention to proper posture and our conversation employs the same strategy of considerateness and a number of intricate polite phrases, some of which are not easy to explain (e.g., "You *must* have another piece of this cake").

Obviously, the differences that exist are differences in degree and emphasis. In the Japanese system of politeness, participants do more or less the same things, but they may be doing them more often. Also, as already mentioned above, the fact that someone is senior or junior, in-group or out-group, and male or female plays a much more basic role in the communication system. However, it is questionable whether in the world of socioeconomic interaction the distinction between the Japanese and foreigners is still as convincing as in the world of communication behavior.

Politeness in Contact Situations

The communication of politeness belongs to those sectors of communication that are likely to be most strongly, and adversely, affected by the conditions of contact situations. One aspect of the problem is that native speakers in contact situations often stick to their norms quite consistently. For instance, speakers frequently believe that their own rules of etiquette are "natural" and that someone who does not adhere to the same system is impolite. Violations of politeness rules are thus sometimes due to interference from the other system of etiquette.

Let me give a few examples from the area of table manners. Although this will rarely happen, a Japanese participant may lift his plate while eating soup. This can be explained as a case of influence from the Japanese system of table manners, which prescribes that when soup is eaten the bowl is lifted up.

However, sometimes new rules are created. For instance, when wine is being served, some Japanese participants lift their glass. This can result in a lack of balance of the glass and in the spilling of wine on the tablecloth. There is no rule to this effect in the Japanese system of etiquette, and the trend can be explained as an analogy from the Japanese custom of pouring saké or beer for one's companions. Also, some cases of violation of politeness rules may derive from "simplification" of behavior, due to the loss of control. A Japanese who is struggling with his basic grammar and vocabulary while speaking with his neighbor may easily forget to reciprocate when the neighbor pours a drink for him.

Foreigners who appear in situations in which Japanese norms prevail do not fare better. They may eat too quickly (to give the impression of being hungry is bad), in incorrect order, drop things held in their chopsticks, etc. A restriction that only recently started being relaxed is eating while walking. In Japan, people used to eat their ice cream in the shop where they bought it. To walk while licking an ice cream cone used to invite condescending looks from disgusted passers-by, and sometimes still does. To buy a doughnut and eat it in front of the shop will often be watched with amazement. However, those rules have more recently been breaking down, in particular with regard to eating in outside areas that are singled out for relaxation (parks, shopping areas from which traffic has been excluded, etc.).

Violation of norms in general is not easy to correct for native speakers and this is particularly true about violations of the rules of etiquette. It is difficult for a native speaker to point to a foreigner making even a grammatical mistake, but to effectively tell someone "You are being rude" is as difficult to do in Japanese as it is in English. This is one of the reasons why even after an exposure to contact situations for a considerable duration of time some foreigners may retain their "bad" habits. To remove them, they should not ask for correction of their own behavior. It is better to phrase the questions as general questions, asking what a Japanese would do in particular situations. Such questions are easily answered without the danger of being directly and offensively impolite. Of course, when we ask questions about etiquette, we must think of the broad variation between native speakers and select a speaker who is likely to possess good judgment on the type of situations we want to know about.

MESSAGE FORM RULES: HOW TO ORDER COMPONENTS OF COMMUNICATION ACTS

Even if we know what content will be communicated, through what variety of language, to whom, when, and where, we still face the problem of how to actually arange all that we want to communicate into a sequence. The problem is the same as knowing what words we want to use in a sentence and what their relationship should be, but not knowing in what order they should be used to form a meaningful sentence. However, in the present section we shall not be able to discuss the arrangement of words in sentences; our major concern will be the order (sequencing or arrangement) of speech acts within communication encounters and the use of "routine" components in which both the content and ordering of elements have been fixed.

The Letter Case

The concept of message form can be further exemplified by the communicative genre we call a letter. A letter normally contains information of various kinds. Of course, the factual content we want to transmit tends to be of primary importance, but further information of various types is normally included. For instance, it is usual to include information about the addressee (name, address, etc.), about the sender (name, address), and about the setting of the act of producing the letter. Letters may also include additional information not connected with the factual content of the letter but usual in the system of communication (greetings, thanks, apologies, comments about the weather, etc.). What will be communicated is decided on the basis of content rules, which are specific for a particular language, and within that language for the particular category of letters. For instance, business letters in English do not usually contain reference to the season of the year, while in Japanese they often do. Private letters in English obligatorily include an "addressing phrase" (Dear Charlie, etc.) while private Japanese letters usually give only the name of the addressee (and then, only at the end of the letter).

The arrangement of content within a letter is also different in different systems of communication, and this is certainly true about letters both in Japanese and in English. Let us consider only one type of letters: "business letters" written by an individual and addressed to another individual within an organization.

First, the distribution of information that appears on the envelope and inside the letter somewhat differs. In English, the sender's address is normally on the envelope but the information is also repeated within the letter itself. On the other hand, in Japanese the address of the sender is not normally noted in the letter; it is, however, an obligatory component of the text on the envelope. It is sometimes felt that even for information about the name of the sender the envelope is the more appropriate place. Although this does not happen very often, there are letters that do not carry any explicit identification of the sender within the letter itself. Even if the letter is signed "Satō" there are so many Satōs that the writer may be virtually unidentifiable. Letters in Japan are therefore filed together with their envelopes. As I shall mention later, this has important consequences for contact situations.

Within a business letter, the text itself commences in English with the address of the sender and the date. In Japanese business letters, the address, as just mentioned, does not appear in the letter itself, and the date appears at the end of the letter. Instead of the sender's address, some Japanese letters may have an indication where the letter was actually written (and this may be different from the address of the sender on the envelope), but such information also appears at the end of the letter. Note that this type of letter will normally be written in horizontal lines rather than in the traditional vertical columns. Further, English business letters normally give the address of the addressee in the left upper corner, but this again is missing in the case of Japanese letters. The name of the addressee appears, however, at the end of the letter. In general one can perhaps speak of the strategy to place other than factual content at the beginning of the letter in English, and at the end of the letter in Japanese.

Strictly speaking, what information appears in the addressing phase is more a matter of selecting the proper content rather than arranging it, but I cannot resist the temptation to mention this problem here. First, in the same way as on the European continent, Japanese business letters to organizations are normally addressed to the organization itself, and not to a particular person within the organization. In English, I normally address enquiries and other correspondence to the head of the office concerned, or when the name is not known, the letter can be addressed to "The Secretary," "The Manager," or simply, "Dear Sir." Japanese speakers who are instructed to address their application to Mr. J. Large, Head, Department of Public Works, . . . sometimes believe that the person really receives the letter. In fact, this is a formal matter and the letter normally goes straight to the desk of Mr. Little who handles the particular agenda for Mr. Large. In Japanese, the letter would be addressed simply "To the Department of Public Works." Secondly, considerable care is given by educated English speakers to the selection of the address. Many Japanese writers of English letters believe that the general title Mr./Mrs./Miss is good enough to address everyone, but in most English-speaking communities, addressees with more specialized titles (Dr., Major General, Reverend, etc.) are normally addressed with that title. The title Ms. has also become very common, at least in America, Canada, and Australia. Moreover, many people feel that they should be addressed with their (title and) name, rather than with the formal (and impersonal) substitute "Sir" or "Madam." With regard to the actual form of the addressing phrase, it is important that it normally only has three "slots": the word "dear" (which is used without hesitation even to people we hate), the title (omitted before first names), and one name. Notice in addition that the use of abbreviations and periods is also meaningful. For instance, Dr. is almost always abbreviated, while to abbreviate professor to Prof. is less polite than to write it in full. Some people prefer Mr/Mrs/Ms to Mr./Mrs./Ms.. To write Miss. (with a period) is simply wrong. Since there are no abbreviations in our sense in Japanese, none of the problems is familiar to the average Japanese speaker.

An English letter often ends with a formula such as "Yours," "Yours sincerely," or "Yours truly," and although these expressions, when used, do not convey any "factual information," they do speak of the writer's social outlook, attitudes, and the interpretation of his/her relationship with the addressee. In Japanese, there are short expressions similar to these which mean almost nothing, such as *keigu* (literally, "the instrument of your esteem") or *kashiko* (literally, "obediently," used by female writers only); in addition there are other expressions that are used at the beginning of the letter such as *zenryaku* (literally, "omitting front [greetings]").

Letter Form in Contact Situations

When the Japanese write business letters in English they often experience considerable problems in giving the letter the proper form. They may not realize that in Western offices the envelope is often opened by a secretary and disposed of, and that this may result in an irrevocable loss of the address, or even the very identity of the sender. The selection of the proper addressing phrase and the closing phrase is of course difficult. For example, I sometimes receive letters from colleagues addressed "Dear Professor Doctor Jiří Václav Neustupný" and closed with "Yours faithfully," which does not fit the character of the letter at all. Since to correctly "form" a letter is a sign of education in English, many English speakers who receive a letter without the sender's address, addressed in a funny way, and possibly with strange references to the weather, lose both their tempers and the willingness to reply.

Not all problems in letters written by the Japanese in English are caused by interference from Japanese. Some are simply the result of loss of control over the content of the letter (simplification) due to their switch to English. When we switch to an unfamiliar language, we often lose the ability to correctly arrange information into "logical" sequences, may repeat, restart, and make unnecessary detours. This is also one of the problems that appears in English letters written by Japanese speakers.

A number of problems are characteristic for foreigners who write letters in Japanese, including writing the envelope in Japanese characters. One of the first problems which must be tackled is the arrangement of lines on the envelope. In romanization, it is normal to use the Western order, for example:

> Mrs. Norie Tanaka
> 15-4 Yabumachi 1-chome
> (or: 1-15-4 Yabumachi)
> Migi-ku
> Yamanashi-shi 975

When you write the address in characters, the order should be consistently from a larger unit to a smaller, starting with the postal code number:

> 975 Yamanashi-shi, Migi-ku
> Yabumachi 1-15-4
> Tanaka Norie sama

Although it is not impossible today to write the address horizontally, it will normally be written vertically. Then the question of where each line should start, what should be on a separate line and what should be written larger and what smaller becomes a real problem. It is not merely important in order to make the address maximally legible for the postman, but also because a particular pattern of arrangement is usual in Japanese. Readers should understand that further similar issues await the learner when they approach the text proper, but this chapter cannot discuss further details of such problems.

It must also be noted that under the conditions of a contact situation, for instance, when the addressee is a foreigner, or in the case of a Japanese who lives overseas or possesses experience of contact with foreign addressees, various adaptations to the indigenous Japanese pattern occur. For instance, the name of the addressee can move to the front of the letter and constitute a quasi-"addressing phrase." Note, however, that writing in horizontal lines (rather than in vertical columns) is quite usual in native situations as well, and cannot therefore be classified as a feature of contact situations.

It may be useful to add a note here on the order of Japanese personal names: in Japanese the family name precedes the given name, for example, Mishima Yukio. Except for historical names (which often have a different structure), the common practice in European languages is to reverse the order (i.e., Yukio Mishima). However, some Japanese organizations use the Japanese order with the result that foreigners who do not know the language are often completely at a loss as to which is the family name and which is the given name.

Opening and Closing Routines

The issue of ordering components of a message into one sequence is of importance at any stage of generating communicative acts. However, as we could see in the case of letters, of particular interest are the beginnings and ends of encounters, for which some fixed routine expressions (such as the "addressing phrase" or "closing phrase") are available.

The same pattern can be observed in spoken encounters. The telephone is perhaps one example. A formalized and strictly arranged sequence of routines is characteristic both for the opening and the closing of telephone conversations and even though details are different in different speech communities, the principle is shared by all communication systems. In the case of the telephone, such routines perform a practical function, but on many other occasions the ceremonial openings and closings primarily communicate politeness.

In the preceding sections I referred already to the *aisatsu* acts which occur at the beginning and ends of visits. The principle is generally applicable in Japanese. As Takeshi Shibata observed, many Japanese greetings apply in pairs: one at the beginning of an encounter, another one at its end. For instance:

start of daily cycle	*o-hayō gozaimasu* "good morning"
end of daily cycle	*o-yasumi nasai* "good night"
beginning of an irregular encounter	*o-hayō gozaimasu/ konnichi wa/konban wa* (or its equivalent) "hello"
end of irregular encounter	*sayonara* (or its equivalent) "goodbye"
entering someone's office	*shitsurei shimasu* "excuse me"
leaving someone's office	*shitsurei shimashita*
commencing a meal	*itadakimasu*
finishing a meal	*gochisō-sama deshita*

When people leave in the morning and come back to their homes, special pairs of greetings apply:

leaving	*itte mairimasu* (or its equivalent)
returning	*tadaima*

The replies of those who are in the house (but are not leaving) are *itte-rasshai* (or equivalent) on leaving and *o-kaeri nasai* (or equivalent) on the return of the one who had left.

In general, it is necessary to realize that the *aisatsu* routines are not single expressions but that they obligatorily consist of two parts: the "initiation" by one speaker and the "response" by the other. In the case of *o-hayō gozaimasu,* both speakers use the same words. However, as we have seen above, in the case of *itte mairimasu,* the correct reply is different (*itte-rasshai*). Florian Coulmas therefore suggested that such routines should consistently be thought of as pairs consisting of an initiation and a reply.

Differences between English and Japanese Greetings

Since in many Japanese language textbooks most Japanese greetings are given single English equivalents, foreigners are sometimes misled to believe that apart from their number being larger, the Japanese expressions correspond more or less exactly to what is given as their English meaning. However, this assumption is mostly incorrect: not because Japanese would be a "totally different" language, but because any language differs from any other in the repertoire of its routines. The English "Good morning" is used differently from the German "Guten Morgen," and there is no equivalent in French; neither does the English "Hello" or "Good day" correspond exactly to the German "Guten Tag" or the French "Bonjour." Thus, even languages that are as close to each other as the Western European languages do not overlap with regard to the usage of greetings.

Japanese greetings have been described in an admirable fashion in Nobuko and Osamu Mizutani's *Nihongo Notes* and it is therefore not necessary to devote much space to them here. I shall restrict myself to a summary of some of the main features that cause problems in contact situations.

1. The time when the greeting is used

In general *o-hayō gozaimasu* is used in a way similar to the English "good morning." However, the time of the morning when it ceases being applicable is much earlier than in the case of "good morning." The English greeting extends until 12 noon, while the Japanese routine is used roughly until about 10 A.M. You will hear stories about bar hostesses going to work at 6 P.M. and greeting each other with *o-hayō gozaimasu*, but these are special cases and do not constitute a rule for early-rising citizens.

In the case of the Japanese who live overseas, *o-hayō gozaimasu* is one of the language forms that is most readily influenced by English and other languages. In overseas Japanese usage, the range of applicability frequently extends to cover the same period as "good morning" and its equivalents.

2. *The situation in which the greeting applies*

Typical problematic examples are *konnichi wa* and *konban wa*. At overseas universities, students of Japanese often use *konnichi wa* when they meet their teachers, for instance, in the corridor of the departmental area. Some Japanese teachers will accept this pattern but many feel that it is strange. The reason is that *konnichi wa* and *konban wa* do not mark the beginning of a situation which regularly recurs, such as a working situation, or a home situation. When I return home in the evening and say *konban wa*, my children laugh: they know that this can only be a joke. *Konban wa* is not used at home. *Konnichi wa* and *konban wa* are only employed in what can be called "irregular" encounters, that is, encounters which do not recur.

Learners of Japanese often ask what greeting then do the Japanese use if they arrive in their office late, in the afternoon. In situations like that the speakers must improvise: one can say for instance *Osoku narimashita* "Sorry to be late," make a routine remark about the weather such as *Atsui desu ne* "It's hot today, isn't it," or simply bow. The bow is the most general form of greeting and fits perfectly almost any situation. It not only obligatorily accompanies any verbal greeting, but can fully replace it.

By the way, neither *konnichi wa* nor *konban wa* are very formal greetings. We often see in the hotels of Tokyo, New York, Munich, or Sydney Western businessmen who shower visiting senior Japanese colleagues with *Konnichi wa, Tanaka-san* "Hello, Mr. Tanaka," or *konban wa, Yoshida-san* "Good evening, Mr. Yoshida." Of course, one problem here is that unlike in English (or in French), names are not used with greetings in Japanese. That applies to *o-hayō gozaimasu*, as well as to *konnichi wa*, and all the others. However, the situation also is strange because *konnichi wa* and *konban wa* are casual expressions and in Japanese are avoided if the age or status distance between the participants is too great.

The use of Japanese greetings by foreign speakers often can "break the ice" and create a friendly atmosphere. However, some Japanese may feel quite uneasy or even assume a negative attitude if the greeting is used incorrectly. Discuss your own usage with your Japanese friends and if you are not sure, you'd better use English. Your Japanese contacts will normally be glad to have the opportunity to practice what they had learned at school. Greetings are an area in which they normally feel more confident than in other communicative situations.

The greeting *sayonara* "goodbye", often very popular with foreign learners of Japanese, is not easy to use. It marks the end of encounters, but it is difficult to define in a simple way what type of encounters. Only one matter is clear: it is not a greeting suitable for formal or semi-formal situations. Also, it seems that the range of its application is currently undergoing a change in Japan. Foreigners would certainly like to have a single greeting for concluding encounters, but unfortunately there is none. Some Japanese speakers also feel in the same way, but they must use ad hoc replacements such as *ja* (well then), *ja mata* (well then, [let's meet] again), or *dōmo* "very much. . ." . The last item is a useful phrase because of its ambiguity: the speaker doesn't say "very much. . ." what. It can be an abbreviation for *dōmo arigatō gozaimashita* (thank you very much), *dōmo shitsurei shimashita* (I am very sorry), or something similar. *Dōmo* can be used to terminate almost any situation. As in the case of many other greetings, the shade of its meaning will be strongly influenced by the intonation with which it is pronounced.

Note again that the situation of leaving the place where you live (or often where you work) and returning there has a separate set of greetings (*Itte mairimasu*, etc.). When you stay with a Japanese family for some time, you do not say *sayonara* when you leave the house, and you do not say *konnichi wa* or *konban wa* when you return. Foreign students who study in Japan usually pick up the appropriate routines quite easily. Any person who departs calls out *Itte mairimasu* (or its equivalent) from the front door and all people in the house who can hear him or her call back *Itte-irassai*. The greetings are of course exchanged at the normal level of voice if someone sees you off to the entrance. When you return, you open the door and call out *Tadaima*; the reply from those who are in the house will be *O-kaeri nasai* (or its equivalent).

3. *The degree of politeness*

In the preceding section I often used the expression "or its equivalent." This mostly refers to greetings that are differentiated with regard to the degree of politeness they convey. Strictly speaking, the differentiation is a matter of content rules but I shall mention it here.

Some greetings only have one form: *konnichi wa*, *konban wa*, *sayonara*, and *tadaima* belong to this group. However, many are differentiated depending on who the addressee is. The longer form is invariably the more polite one and is used to seniors. The shorter form is used to juniors or to in-group participants of equal status. For instance:

Longer form	Shorter form
o-hayō gozaimasu	*o-hayō*
o-yasumi nasai	*o-yasumi*
itte mairimasu (or *kimasu*)	*itte kuru yo* (or *wa*)
o-kaeri nasai	*o-kaeri*

The differentiation is of considerable importance. Foreign exchange students in Japan sometimes acquire only the shorter forms and use them with everyone. Such usage may be tolerated by in-group participants, but out-group Japanese may think that the student is surpassing all limits of reasonability.

Thanks and Apologies

The same difference between a longer and a shorter form is also present in the simple expression for thanks. The full form is *arigatō gozaimasu* (or *arigatō gozaimashita*, when the thanks are for something that already belongs to the past). The short form is *arigatō*. Notice again that the name of the addressed person is never appended. The short form can be heard very frequently from foreign immigration or customs officers, taxi drivers, hotel employees, shop attendants who probably only know this Japanese word and want to surprise and please Japanese customers. Some Japanese addressees do not mind or will be genuinely pleased. However, the effect can be exactly the opposite. *Arigatō* is all right within your family, to your close friends, to a taxi driver, but not to an out-group senior person. For some Japanese speakers, it can be an irritating experience if they are told just simply *arigatō*.

Florian Coulmas has shown that thanks and apologies in Japanese are intricately connected. Instead of *arigatō gozaimasu* the speaker can also say *sumimasen* (or *sumimasen deshita*, if reference is to an act that already belongs to the past), "I am sorry." The reply is the same both for thanks and apologies: *iie* "no, (not at all)" or in a formal situation *dō itashimashite*. Of course, there are expressions for stronger apologies, but we cannot discuss them in detail. Note also that the expression of thanks differs depending on the situation. For instance, thanks for a coffee or a meal are *gochisō-sama deshita*, etc. However, the phrase *arigatō gozaimashita* can replace any of the more specialized expressions.

Thanks or apologies are obligatory at the beginning of each en-counter which connects with another previous encounter of the same participants, supposing that one of the participants did a favor for another or that one of them was inconvenienced. For instance, if you met Mr. Shimada, and he took you to dinner, the next time you meet him you must acknowledge your gratitude right after the general greetings are over. The Japanese language has a special set of routines for this, for instance, *Senjitsu wa, dōmo arigatō gozaimashita* (Thank you for the other day). When you met Mrs. Nakamura a few days ago and the meeting took too much of her time, you apologize, saying *Senjitsu wa, shitsurei shimashita* (The other day I was impolite).

These routine expressions sometimes cause problems even for foreigners with a considerable fluency in the Japanese language. The reason is obvious: there are no similar expressions in most other languages, and the speaker must carefully control himself not to forget. This is not easy to do if so many other things are to be at-tended to at the beginning of encounters.

A similar problem arises in the case of encounters that have been interrupted. For instance, you speak with Mr. Takebe and are called away to take a telephone call. To mark the beginning of the inter-ruption you will say *Shitsurei shimasu* (Excuse me). This is also com-mon in English. When you resume your position after the telephone call is over, you should say *O-matase shimashita* (I'm sorry to have kept you waiting). This is not perhaps quite unusual for English speakers, but in Japanese, the routine is quite obligatory. Note that since these expressions are apologies, the answer is *iie* or *dō itashimashite*.

Introductions

At the beginning of an encounter in which there are participants unknown to each other, speech acts called "introductions" are used. The whole introduction sequence, if we also include the speech of the person who is introducing, is quite complicated. Let us consider only the routines used by each of the participants who are being introduced. The first component of the basic self-introduction routine is *hajimemashite*, "how do you do." Literally it means "it is for the first time . . ." and, textbook claims notwithstanding, it is the component which can most easily be omitted. The second component is the participant's own name, always pronounced in Japanese, not in English, to which the suffix *-san* ("Mr./Mrs./Miss") is *never* attached. Finally comes the routine *dōzo yoroshiku*, literally "please, kindly . . ." and a bow. This final routine and the bow are very important and if anything is to be left out, it is perhaps the name, but not this closing part.

The exchange of name cards is quite common, not merely in the case of business people, but in social contact as well. Even students and socially active housewives may have name cards, and it is only very recently that one can meet more important people who do not use name cards. Foreigners whose contacts with Japan are of a more permanent nature are well advised to print their own cards with English text on one side and Japanese text on the other. Participants have their card ready before the introductions and are careful about the way the card is handed over and received. As far as practicable both hands are used, the card of the other participant is inspected, and kept before the recipient for some time before being (carefully and mostly at an unnoticed moment) put away.

The Japanese and English Greetings

It might be expected that with the great variety of greetings in their own system of communiction the Japanese will not find it difficult to use English greetings correctly in contact situations. However, this is not necessarily the case. One reason is that the correspondence between the Japanese and English greetings is rather complicated. Another reason is that at school the Japanese are taught particular routines that may not be the most suitable in all English-speaking communities. For instance, most Japanese have been taught to use, when being introduced, the routine "how do you do," which sounds very formal in most contemporary varieties of English. Furthermore, the phenomenon of simplification may appear again: when there are so many things to think of, it is easy to drop a greeting.

Like many other foreigners, the Japanese often overuse the thanks and apologies routines. They say "thank you" and "I am sorry" too often, even when native speakers of English would not use these phrases. On the other hand, the daily greetings often remain unused, with other people wondering what they did wrong to deserve Mrs. Nakamura's refusal to return their "good morning." It might be that Mrs. Nakmura is too shy to speak loudly enough in English to be heard. She did say "good morning" but couldn't be heard. Another frequent case is that instead of the verbal greeting the Japanese bow was actually used but remained unnoticed by other participants.

CHANNEL RULES: HOW MESSAGES ARE TRANSMITTED

Messages can be transmitted in various ways. We can use the spoken language or write. When we write, many possibilities are open: handwriting, typing, printing. Often we transmit messages by using the tone of voice, laughter, or a simple gesture. Of course, our movements, the physical position we occupy in the encounter, our dress, and use of various objects (for instance, a cigarette or a pencil) can also communicate facts about our personality, attitudes, and intentions. Again, there is considerable cross-cultural variation in the use of channels and the specific conditions of their use in contact situations.

Speaking and Writing in Japanese

Students of Japanese sometimes only discover the real importance of the written channel of Japanese after they arrive in Japan. I am not referring to the fact that without the knowledge of Japanese writing it is difficult to travel, shop, and often drink and eat. What perhaps matters more is the lack of access to newspapers, and the extremely rich world of publication which is totally closed to people who cannot read. Some surveys conducted in Japan show that reading is the most favoured activity for most interviewed. In order to participate in social and cultural life in Japan and to join conversations in Japanese networks the use of the written channel, at least a competence in reading, if not in writing, is essential.

Comparative studies of the use of the written and spoken channels in Japan and elsewhere are unavailable. If they existed, they would probably demonstrate that the Japanese read more for entertainment and general information than the average American or European does. Even if there may be some decline in the overall extent of reading, the written medium still remains of great importance. The huge Japanese publishing industry with books, paperbacks, and an enormous variety of monthly and particularly weekly magazines caters for these needs. Reading is the standard activity when there is nothing else to do: people who wait or who travel on the train read. The Japanese also read avidly for further education. A large number of paperback editions are cheaply available for this purpose. They also take more notes, as already noted above, and perhaps write more letters and postcards. This is not changed by the fact that the use of the telephone is widespread both for private and business communication.

On the other hand, in some situations the written channel is used less frequently than in English. For instance, the genre of business correspondence is much less developed. There are of course many documents, reports, and particularly fill-in forms, but Japanese organizations less frequently employ letters or even informal memoranda either of an internal nature or addressed to people outside the company. Negotiations are normally conducted through the spoken channel and only the most important and final points are sealed by a written document. Another interesting pattern is that people in high positions do not necessarily read many documents. When there is an important matter to know about, they are briefed by a junior employee of the company. Briefing of course also exists in Western organizations but my claim is that it plays a much more important role in Japan.

In many countries the necessity to use the written channel for public and business correspondence has led to the development of the institution called "the secretary." Secretaries physically produce documents in the written language and keep them on behalf of other members of staff; however, they do not normally produce and sign documents of their own. In Japanese organizations, real secretaries in this sense are rare. There are low-paid female clerical workers for the odd job and to make tea or coffee. But in principle everyone works on a separate task, and even people in high positions may write their letters and other documents themselves. It is only with the advent of the word processor that professional typists have come to be employed in larger numbers.

Typing and Word Processing in Japan

Since the number of symbols to select from when producing even an average document in Japanese is about 3,000, to type is not a task comparable to typing in English with just about 50 standard symbols. The most common type of a conventional Japanese typewriter does not have a keyboard. The symbols are kept on a board from which they are picked by the typist with a movable bridge to be subsequently pressed against the roller, as on an English typewriter. Then the symbol is returned to its place. Understandably, the process is slow: even in the case of an experienced professional typist the time needed is comparable to the time used by a rather inexperienced, unprofessional typist in English.

To achieve efficiency, some organizations, for instance, the gas or telephone companies, are using *kana* typewriters with only a few characters for sending out their periodical bills. In this case the speed of writing is even faster than in English, but since the documents produced in this way are not real Japanese documents (no real Japanese texts are written only in *kana*), *kana* typewriters can only be used for limited purposes. Some telex terminals provide *kana* printouts, even though the use of romanization in telex is widespread.

When the use of computers for word processing started, many people believed that now the time had come when Japan would have to finally romanize its writing system. However, the computers quickly learned how to work with characters. Today, word processing programs are available for Japanese, and word processors are quickly replacing the old typewriters. Many individuals are using word processors for writing letters and producing other documents in Japanese. There are many methods of input, the most common by typing each word in *kana* (or in romanization) and subsequently converting those parts of the word that should be written with a character into the character. When it is necessary to select one of several characters that are pronounced identically, such characters appear on the screen and the typist simply selects the correct one by pushing the "convert" key. Typing on a word processor is slower (and will probably remain slower) than typing in English, but for professional typists the difference is not prohibitive and a reasonable speed can be achieved even by untrained individuals. Although handwriting may be faster, word processing makes available correction facilities and storage of the text for future use.

Literacy in Japan

How competent are the Japanese in using the written channel of communication? Official statistics give the rate of literacy in Japan as virtually 100 percent, but can the figures be trusted? The answer is that although the figure given is virtually worthless, the literacy rate in Japan has been amazingly high, in particular if the character of the script, one of the most difficult of all ages and all languages, is taken into consideration. No doubt, the fact that the Japanese are such enthusiastic readers (and writers) provides an important support for literacy in Japan.

What are the exact literacy figures? The answer is that no exact figures can be given, either for Japan or for any other country. One reason is that literacy is a matter of degree; another reason is that sophisticated and reliable surveys are extremely rare. In Japan two excellent surveys were conducted, but the last one refers to the period 1955-56. The investigation was conducted for a sample of young Japanese in two selected areas, Tokyo and a rural area of northern Japan, and revealed that the total percentage of illiterates was less than one percent in either of the two areas, but this figure referred only to people who had no competence whatsoever in reading *kana* and basic characters. However, ten percent of the Tokyo sample and more than fifteen percent of the rural sample were persons who were expected by the researchers to experience serious problems in the use of the written language. Approximately fifty to sixty percent of the total population were judged to face some problems. This situation is probably not very different from that in other advanced industrial countries: absolute illiteracy is of course very low, but it can be assumed that even today at least ten percent of the total adult population is likely to suffer from serious problems in the use of written documents in their daily life.

Gestures and their Social Significance

While the oral and the written channels are typically used in verbal communication, gestures and many other "paralinguistic," "kinesic," spatial and other patterns belong to what is normally called non-verbal behavior. This is a broad and important area, in particular for the transmission of other than factual information.

Gestures are a type of Japanese non-verbal behavior that have been described in a considerable number of publications. In these writings we can find out how to indicate with a gesture the concept of "money," "be out of one's mind," and many others. One fact which is not normally mentioned is that there are social constraints on the use of such gestures. None of them is considered a very refined means of communications, and some are clearly marked by many Japanese speakers as vulgar. It is good to know all of them, but to employ them actively is a different matter.

Even to point to objects with your finger is not considered to be the most elegant way of drawing attention. Normally, a verbal descriptor can be used. When it is necessary to employ a pointing gesture, the whole hand can be used with the palm up. This is the method used in Japan by tourist bus guides who have to indicate to their customers in what direction they should turn. However, the speaker can point to oneself with the forefinger, but the finger is directed to one's nose, not to the chest as in most European systems of communication. Mizutani relates a hilarious story of a teacher of Japanese who introduced himself to a beginner's class with *Watashi wa sensei desu* (I am [your] teacher), pointing to his nose. Half of the class believed that the sentence meant "This is my nose."

Laughing and Smiling

The new stereotype of the Japanese implicitly suggests that they do not laugh. They do, and quite a lot. Since no detailed studies of the Japanese laughter exist, it is difficult to say whether and in what way it differs from the way the Americans or anyone else laughs. Suggestions have been made that the Japanese laughter is more sub-dued and does not tolerate the eruptive style, which certainly exists in the West. Some Japanese do certainly feel that the laughter of some foreign female speakers is too explosive and loud. However, the opinion of the Japanese here is divided. By many, the liveliness of the Western facial expression is evaluated in a positive way; others feel that "too much is too much." The same division of opinion also exists with regard to laughter. Young Japanese often laugh, as we would say, quite "freely," without worrying about any traditional cultural constraints.

Smiling resembles laughing, except that it is unaccompanied by voice. In most systems of communication smiling communicates friendliness, but it can also indicate embarassment and other types of emotion. There seem to be some differences between Japanese smil-ing and smiling when using European languages. In English and other languages we use similing to accentuate certain points in our discourse. In other words, the smile is put on, is extinguished (to communicate that we are serious), and goes on again. In Japanese a speaker may "put on" a smile at the beginning of a discourse and re-tain it for a very long time. English-speaking participants in the en-counter often feel that his speech is monotonous and perhaps that he is insincere. The stereotype picture of the "inscrutable Japanese" normally has two faces: one which is deadly serious and one which smiles.

The complaint that one could read little from the Japanese facial expression used to be very common overseas. However, in the less conservative system of Japanese communication this is not true any more. Fewer and fewer constraints are placed on the expression of emotions and the results can be clearly seen in the case of both children and adults.

Nose Blowing

My attention has been drawn to the issue of nose blowing by a number of exchange students who studied for a period of one year at Japanese high schools. They said that the first time they took out their handkerchief and blew their nose, there was an outburst of laughter in their class. First, in Japan disposable tissues are used; the handkerchief is used to wipe one's hands, sweat, and for various other purposes, but not for nose cleaning; to use it to wipe one's nose is seen as an unclean habit. Secondly, the act of nose cleaning is performed in Japan out of sight of others. This is why it often escapes the attention of foreigners, some of whom then continue to embarrass their environment with the wiping act and to amuse it with the sound which accompanies their use of the handkerchief.

Touching and the Handshake

In general, we can say that people in Japan do rarely intentionally touch each other. Of course, one cannot avoid touching other people in crowded places (transport, street, public spaces) and normally apologies are not issued under such circumstances. Occasionally you will also be able to observe women touching men's knees, for instance when reacting to a joke. However, people do not put their arms around other people's shoulders, and although young people do not normally feel any hesitation walking hand in hand in public, for the older generation even such behavior may be socially marked.

When greeting each other the Japanese have never used the embrace, to say nothing of kissing, or a handshake. Today the handshake is fully familiar to those people who possess the experience of contacts with foreigners. However, there are Japanese who hesitate to shake hands. It is always necessary to watch carefully and to help in moments of indecision. Occasionally it is possible to meet Japanese who are not absolutely sure about the distance between speakers when shaking hands, the length of the handshake, and its intensity. Again, it is not improper for the foreigner to take the initiative on similar occasions.

The Bow

The Japanese bow subsumes the same function as the Western handshake but, as mentioned above, its application is much wider: it accompanies virtually all verbal greetings and can replace almost any of them. The bow has many degrees, with the lowest and most polite variety called *saikeirei*. This variety is not used, except when a special degree of respect is in place. A casual, light bow is called *eshaku.* One normally executes a bow in a stationary position, standing or sitting on the floor, but there are varieties appropriate for walking or for sitting on a chair. It is very important to realize that the bow in the standing position, which is the basic type of the bow for a foreign speaker, has a different form for men (who put their arms along their body) and women (who join their hands in front of them).

The basic problem for foreigners who speak Japanese is that they do not bow when they are expected to. As emphasized before, a bow accompanies all greetings and is a response to all offers, compliments, and a number of other behavioral patterns. To say *Arigatō gozaimashita* "Thank you" and not to bow is strange. Native speakers of Japanese may not be able to immediately say what causes the feeling of strangeness, but they will clearly perceive the incongruence of the situation. The reason for omitting the bow is mostly lack of competence. However, in the case of some learners of Japanese, there is the false feeling that the bow means a very high degree of politeness, as it sometimes does in the person's native system of communication. This is silly. In the context of Japanese communication the bow is a neutral tool which does not convey a particularly high degree of politeness, to say nothing about flattery or subservience. Of course, the extreme bow (*saikeirei*) does have special connotations and should not be used unless appropriate for the situation.

It is not easy for the Japanese to remove the bow when they speak English. Sometimes it appears, is noticed, and is interpreted as a sign of special politeness. Much of the impression of the foreigner that the Japanese are so polite probably derives from the retention of the bow by many speakers of Japanese in contact situations.

How to Sit

The Japanese sitting posture is normally more "classical" than the Western one, whether they sit on a chair or on the floor (tatami). The position of one's legs and arms is subject to more constraints. For instance, at a concert most people will sit straight with their hands on their knees or in their lap. Leaning against one side, or sitting too low in the chair communicates much more informality than it normally would in America or in Europe. Further, many Japanese now cross their legs when sitting on a chair and no special meaning is attributed to the fact. However, in the more conservative system junior participants should not cross their legs in front of seniors. Readers will be able to check themselves to what extent this rule is applied in situations in which they will participate.

When sitting on the floor there are three basic types of positions. The most formal one is called *seiza* (correct sitting), in which the person sits with legs folded underneath the body. In encounters that take place in a traditional Japanese room (on the tatami), this is the basic posture in which greetings are exchanged. Younger Japanese, who do not normally live on tatami, find this position uncomfortable, and sometimes cannot stand up or walk straight after having assumed it for a long period of time. Of course, it also has a damaging effect on men's trousers. After the greetings are over, the host usually suggests that the guest changes to a more comfortable position. For men this is *agura* (sitting cross-legged). It is very important to realize that women never sit cross-legged. Their informal sitting position is to fold their legs along (rather than underneath) their body.

Some foreigners are afraid of situations which require sitting on the tatami. However, this is not necessary, because the Japanese do normally understand if a foreigner is unable to take the usual Japanese sitting position. Of course, foreigners who speak Japanese are judged more strictly than casual tourists. To exchange Japanese greetings at the beginning or end of an encounter in the *agura* (cross-legged) position is likely to be misinterpreted if the foreigner involved speaks Japanese really well.

How to Eat and Drink

Table manners are closely connected with the social attributes of participants and communicate about their origin, education, and personality. Only a few points which sometimes lead to misunderstanding in contact situations will be mentioned here.

First, in the Japanese sector, many dishes are normally served at the same time. In the case of a Japanese dinner, one starts normally with a sip of the soup, but then picks alternately from various plates and bowls. To finish one dish before proceeding to another is very unusual. Secondly, the soup bowl and the rice bowl are always held in your left hand to facilitate drinking of soup and eating. Thirdly, if you take food from a shared plate, reverse your chopsticks. Fourthly, empty dishes are not removed from the table (the hostess did not "forget to remove them"). Finally, before the Japanese start eating they say *Itadakimasu*, and mostly finish eating with saying *Gochisō-sama deshita*. Meals usually proceed slowly and as mentioned above participants avoid giving the impression that they are hungry and cannot restrain themselves.

Many books for foreigners suggest that slurping is obligatory when eating noodles. It is not, even though it does occur and is totally acceptable. In general, sophisticated people try to eat as quietly as possible.

When a group of people eat together in a restaurant, it is not uncommon that they follow the lead of the most senior participant and order the same dish. A foreigner who is asked by others "what will you have" does not sometimes realize that his choice may have serious consequences for others. This responsibility can be avoided if he returns the same question and manages to be the last to choose.

"Nice guys" are expected to like alcoholic beverages; hence, when you are asked whether you like to drink, the correct answer is "yes." This does not commit anyone to actually drinking, and many Japanese are in fact teetotallers. Nobody is normally pushed into drinking by hosts or friends if he doesn't want to. To look a little drunk or to be actually drunk is not socially taboo, and does not communicate anything about one's personality as it would in most Western and many Asian countries.

Formality of Dress

Dress communicates. Both what is worn and how it is worn communicates about the personality and attitudes of participants in communicative encounters. In contact situations, the problem of the dress moves to the foreground. For instance, problems may arise if the general strategy in one community is to be dressed rather formally, while the other community in contact pays little attention to clothing.

Although not all men in Japan are dressed in dark suits and white shirts and not all women always wear fancy dresses and high-heeled shoes, one can easily discern a great deal of interest in clothes and a certain traditionalism in taste. There is a general sense of need to differentiate according to the situation. I have mentioned already that at wedding parties people are dressed very formally. For playing sports or mountain climbing the "proper" dress is normally worn, and most people can be expected to wear dark dress for a concert. Of course, when a new fashion in female clothes or hair style appears it takes on very quickly and consistently throughout the nation, even if it implies a "casual look." However, temporary predilections for an informal style have not so far completely destroyed the basic Japanese trend toward neatness and balance.

In the case of some foreign participants in contact situations there are definitely problems with regard to dress. When you are invited to dine out with a Japanese family and arrive dressed in a very informal way, this may communicate to the Japanese host that you underestimate the occasion. It can happen that the Japanese family will be dressed very casually, too, but this would be rather exceptional. There is no harm in Japan if you slightly "overdress." Perhaps you may occaionally (though probably seldom) find that your business contacts will be dressed in rather sporty clothes, but you will wish to emphasize the seriousness of your mission by wearing a plain color business suit with an unpretending shirt and a necktie which does not violate the current trends in Japanese necktie fashion.

Presents

The importance of presents in Japanese society has already been mentioned above. Presents communicate politeness, the desire to remain close to a particular person or to newly establish a close relationship. For foreigners, the most common situation to give presents is when they visit a Japanese family, both overseas and in Japan. In the latter case, presents are due to most people you already know and meet again, and especially to people you visit for the first time. Do not hesitate, when you are not sure, to discuss whether, and possibly what kind of, a present should be given with other Japanese friends who are likely to possess a realistic picture of the relationship between yourself and the person involved.

The best present is an object connected with your home country. No doubt, the selection may be difficult in the case of countries that are not as gift-oriented as Japan, and this is almost every country in the world. It is preferable to avoid cheap foreign products that might also be marketed in Japan. Unfortunately, the Japanese often exchange quite expensive presents, so a very cheap or cheap-looking object is unsuitable. Of course, a nominal present will be sufficient in the case of a casual acquaintance. If you could not bring a present with you and are visiting a Japanese family, a box of fruit or unusual pastries, cakes, or imported chocolates will normally make a suitable gift. It is a fact that presents are sometimes passed on to other people, so if your friend hates chocolates he will be able to find an appropriate use for them.

Wrapping is a part of the present. If you buy a box of chocolates in Japan, the shop attendant will ask whether it is a present and wrap the box for you (after removing the price tag) accordingly. If you bring a present from your own country you must make sure that it is properly wrapped.

When handing the present over it is appropriate to say something like "it's absolutely nothing . . . " (e.g., *tsumaranai mono desu ga* . . .) and pass it on, holding it in both hands. To use one hand only for handing things over is impolite. A present is not normally inspected in front of the giver, and unless its price is exceptionally high, there is no need for a separate acknowledgment. Also, presents are not immediately or ostentatiously reciprocated. A receiver must wait for the suitable occasion to repay a kindness. Note finally, that when the Japanese travel, they bring back presents for all their contacts. So a foreign professor may receive a present from his Japanese student who has just returned from Japan. This should be taken as a formality: the present does not commit the professor to pass the student at the annual examinations.

When the value of the present is incommensurable to the situation, the boundary between a gift and a bribe may disappear. Of course, there are bribes in the world of politics and business, and some of them, such as those in the "Lockheed scandal," have become internationally known. However, at the level of daily life, bribes are unthinkable; it is entirely impossible to obtain special treatment by offering money in order to be admitted to a full show or to jump the queue in a full restaurant.

It is a well-known fact that there is no tipping in Japan. People may be offended if a tip is offered. When paying a taxi driver or a hairdresser you may leave the change. The only case where a tip is appropriate is when leaving a Japanese inn (*ryokan*), if you think that some of the personnel was especially kind to you. However, even in this case a gratuity is optional; if you do give money it should be handed over in an envelope or at least wrapped in paper. This applies in all other cases of handing over money, except of course when paying in a shop.

Foreigners and Non-Verbal Communication

Participants in contact situations normally have a task to achieve and if their foreignness is too strongly perceived, this can negatively affect the attainment of their goals. Therefore, it is important for them not to communicate excessively that they are foreigners. Since much of such communication takes place through non-verbal channels, they are interested in being able to control their use of the channels.

There are inborn differences between foreigners. Someone who is two meters tall, blond, and has blue eyes communicates of course by his very presence that he is a foreigner. On the other hand, a slightly built participant with dark hair and a darker eye color will more easily avoid attention. However, even the blue-eyed foreigner may modify the impression he would naturally create if he controls his voice, facial expression, and movements, and if he is dressed in an unobtrusive fashion. The use of artifacts is important. A camera will communicate that you are a tourist, if not a foreigner, and if you carry it, the probability that you will be approached by people who wish to practice English or who wish to make various ''business'' proposals will increase. (In general, this happens in Japan rather seldom.) An important element is gaze. Foreigners who walk through the town obviously looking in all directions (as if asking for help), are much more likely to be approached. If a foreigner enters a coffee shop, looks around in all directions, then sits down in a casual way, joking vividly with his companions, it may happen that the waitresses will gather in one corner and giggle and that nobody will want to come and serve him. The use of non-verbal channels of communication can be observed by people other than those you are communicating with. Hence, if you are breaking Japanese norms of behavior, this will embarrass not only yourself but also your Japanese friends who are with you.

In order to control their non-verbal behavior, participants must know what the Japanese norms are and how they might violate them. I have repeatedly emphasized that the influence of the native system of communication is only one source. In the case of non-verbal behavior the phenomenon of losing control (simplification) is particularly relevant. When speaking in a foreign language participants often lose control over their non-verbal channels. For instance, they can speak too loudly, laugh excessively, gesticulate with their hands and arms, assume strange postures, come too close to their communication partners, etc. All this happens both to the Japanese when they communicate in English and to us when we communicate in Japanese. To know that this can happen is the first step toward improving one's communicative performance.

MANAGEMENT RULES:
HOW WE BEHAVE TOWARD LANGUAGE

Management rules are used to label communication acts in various ways, to assess their correctness, evaluate them, and to improve them when necessary.

Labeling Communicative Acts

The most common labeling of speech in Japanese concerns its regional flavor. In the same way that native speakers of English can label the speech patterns of other speakers as "American English," "British English," "Irish English," "Indian English," etc., the Japanese can label speech as characteristic of particular parts of Japan. This is a component of a speaker's communicative competence, a component that is often missing in foreign speakers of the language. Of course, the precision of differentation depends on the communicative experience of each individual speaker. In general, speakers can distinguish with considerable accuracy where another speaker comes from if the area is close to their domicile. The more distant the area, the less detailed the labeling. For instance, speakers from Kansai can distinguish whether another speaker comes from Kyoto, Osaka, or Kobe, but for a speaker from Kantō (e.g., Tokyo)

all these areas will coincide under a single label, "Kansai." The remaining labels common in the case of Kantō are "Tōhoku" and to
some extent "Kyūshū." Other areas will normally be marked simply as *chihō* "the country." The differentiation is carried out un-
consciously, mainly on the basis of features of pronunciation.
Sometimes, however, listeners are aware of the marked elements: in
the case of Kansai, a typical distinguishing feature is the accent of adjectives on the first syllable (e.g., *áoi* "blue"), in the case of Tōhoku
the pronunciation of certain syllables (e.g., *tsu*), and in the case of
Kyūshū the pronunciation of *se* in the polite ending *-masen* as *she,*
(e.g., *-mashen*). Many speakers also possess some "theoretical"
knowledge of Japanese dialects, for instance they know that the
word "is" (*desu* in the Tokyo dialect) is *dosu* in Kyoto and *dasu* in
Osaka, and that "however" is *batten* in Kyūshū. However, this
"theoretical" knowledge is not necessarily applied in practice when
it comes to listening to regionally colored speech and labeling it.

The existence of labeling of speech is important for foreigners who
are learning Japanese. In no language are foreigners expected to use
regional forms. It is therefore necessary to realize that some features
of the Japanese language are labeled as regionally limited and that
they can be negatively evaluated if used by foreign speakers. For instance, verbal forms ending in *-chatta* (e.g., *itchatta* "went away")
can be labeled as non-standard Tokyo speech by (mainly older)
speakers from other than the Kantō area. In the same way, a number
of features which can unwittingly be acquired by speakers who are
learning Japanese in the Kansai area will be labeled as "Kansai" by
many speakers in other parts of Japan, and negatively evaluated even
by some speakers in the Kansai area itself. This is not to say that
foreigners should carefully avoid areas of Japan other than Tokyo.
The acquisition of negatively evaluated regional forms of Japanese
can easily be avoided if the learner knows what these forms are and
how to replace them by their unlabeled (standard) equivalents.

Social class labels are attached to participants in encounters in the
same way as in any other society of the world. However, while in
some societies the labeling is a conscious process, in Japan many people are unaware of it.

As mentioned above, foreigners are normally marked as
"foreigners" on the basis of their reduced competence in com-

munication and violation of Japanese communicative norms. Such marking is not necessarily an unfriendly act. Often foreigners enjoy a number of privileges, but some foreigners in Japan resent the label and the special treatment which results from it. For instance, participants marked as "foreigners" may be addressed in English even if they want to practice Japanese, and may not be treated as permanent members of networks. As I said above, the only way to avoid such labeling is through reducing the number of one's foreign features and through penetration into Japanese in-group networks. The two conditions are, of course, intimately interrelated.

Communication Norms

All speakers of Japanese possess norms that they apply to their own speech and to the speech of others to assess whether such speech is correct or not. For foreign speakers the existence of norms has special significance even if they do not speak Japanese. The reason is that Japanese speakers often transfer their own norms concerning communication into contact situations. A mistaken expectation of many foreigners is that if the language spoken in a contact situation is English, English communication norms will apply throughout the encounter. For instance, they expect that the setting, participants, or topic will naturally be selected on the basis of English norms. However, this does not necessarily happen.

Japanese speakers do accept that in principle English norms will apply when English is spoken. However, they are often not aware that in many respects they expect foreigners to behave in accordance with Japanese norms. I have mentioned above many instance of such behavior. For example, whether English is spoken or not, foreigners are expected to sit (on a chair) in a formal way and if their posture is too relaxed, this fact may be negatively evaluated. Of course, in some cases foreigners are on the contrary exempted from adhering to Japanese norms: the case of assuming the formal (*seiza*) sitting posture on tatami is an example which was already discussed above. Unfortunately, the question of which Japanese norms are required and which are not has not been systematically described so far. However, it will be useful for foreigners to know that this phenomenon occurs.

Hesitation

An interesting example of "management" of communication is the phenomenon of hesitation. Speakers "hesitate" when they label their own speech as potentially incorrect or while they are planning or replanning what they will say. Sometimes hesitation may be used as a signal that the speaker is highly concerned about the correctness of his or her speech, and is doing his or her best. The ways speakers hesitate are of course specific for individual communication systems.

In Japanese some common hesitation words are *ā, jā, sā, ēto,* and the word *anō.* A typical hesitation which concerns the content of the message is *sō desu ne* (that's right, isn't it). It is necessary to avoid English hesitation words such as "uhuh" because they sound very unnatural in Japanese. A frequent bad habit of foreigners is to hesitate by using the first person pronoun, something like *watashi wa* . . . This, too, is very unusual, because the pronoun is normally only used when absolutely necessary and does not fit in a situation where the speaker is not actually quite sure what to say.

Too much hesitation creates a difficult situation for the listener who becomes easily tired. On the other hand, to speak without any hesitation, as many older textbooks of Japanese de facto recommend, produces a strange effect and certainly communicates strongly the foreignness of the speaker.

How Are Mistakes Handled?

Even native speakers of a language make mistakes, change the plan of their utterances, misunderstand other speakers and ask for explanations. The same is of course true to a much larger extent with foreign speakers in contact situations. Yet, programs which teach English to the Japanese and Japanese to other speakers hardly ever accept this obvious fact.

One major difference between English and Japanese seems to be that while in English requests for repetition and explanation are issued very easily, in Japanese it is somewhat impolite to pursue a senior speaker with questions such as "What did you say?" or "What do you mean?" One result of this is the fact that there is no generally applicable polite routine in Japanese such as the English "Could you please say it again?" which foreigners might use when they ask for repetition. Many foreign speakers of Japanese say *Mō ichido itte kudasai* which does mean "Please say it once more," but it is a strange sentence, to say nothing about the fact that it is not polite enough to be used to out-group addressess.

A more acceptable way to ask for repetition is through the following sequence of acts: (1) hesitate (*ano*), (2) apologize (*sumimasen ga*), (3) explain that you have a comprehension problem (*chotto wakaranakatta n desu*), and (4) ask "what did you say?", using the normal polite expression (*nan to osshaimashita ka*). For speech addressed to out-group juniors or equals or to in-group speakers (including teachers), routine short expressions (*ha?* or *e?* followed by eye contact) exist and can be used.

When the problem is not in correctly hearing a word or a part of a sentence but in the meaning, it has little sense to ask for repetition. In that case a possible informal routine is to repeat the word with an intonation that indicates hesitation (e.g., *shōgun?*). One can also produce a full polite sequence consisting again of hesitation, apology, statement of the problem, and specification of what action is required (e.g., *Shōgun 'tte nan desu ka* "What is 'shogun'?").

After a mistake has actually appeared in one's own speech a correction can of course be made by repeating the correct form. It is then important to repeat a whole "word", not merely a single constituent (even if it happens to be romanized separately, see Chapter IV). For instance when correcting the sentence. "I will go" to "I, too, will go" after having uttered the first "word" *watashi wa . . .* , it is necessary to start again and say *watashi mo* "I, too," because the English word "too" is a dependent suffix in Japanese (*mo*) and cannot be used on its own.

For the correction of a speaker's own speech, hesitation routines, mentioned in the preceding section, are of great importance. If foreign speakers know how to correctly hesitate and subsequently elicit the help of a native speaker, they can pass through a number of encounters for which they do not possess sufficient linguistic means. Some useful routines are for instance *ēto, nan to ittara ii deshō ka* (well, how should I say that?), *eigo de wa 'shisutemu' to iimasu ne* (in English one says 'system'), *taikei deshita-kke* (was it "taikei" [in Japanese]?), *Nihongo de nan to iimasu ka* (how do you say that in Japanese?), etc. If a foreign speaker can successfully operate hesitation and correction routines in Japanese, the impression a native speaker receives is usually very favorable. It pays off to devote attention to these matters even at the very elementary level of competence in the Japanese language.

Can We Learn How to Communicate?

Samuel Martin once commented that a foreigner who memorizes about twenty or thirty common situational exchanges in Japanese can circulate in Japanese society with surprising success. What I have said in this chapter should confirm this claim while adding to Martin's twenty or thirty routines a number of additional rules of communicative competence. As a matter of fact, if we know the rules of communication, perhaps even fewer Japanese language routines will be needed. A casual visitor will be able to communicate in English— subject, of course, to the knowledge of how to communicate in a contact situation with the Japanese.

Throughout this chapter I have often suggested that in situations of contact with the Japanese foreigners are well advised to take into account the fact that Japanese norms are applied and that some adjustment of behavior is needed. Note that we normally expect the Japanese to change their behavior and to communicate and interact as we do when English is spoken. However, many foreigners, even those who are learning the Japanese language, often feel that if they accept the Japanese system of dividing personnel into communicative seniors and juniors, adjust their conversational topics, communicate politeness in the Japanese way or use the bow, they not merely employ a different communication system but also change their personality and identity. People who feel that way are welcome not to change if they realize what they are doing and what the consequences for them are. However, such knowledge is not normally present. Most foreigners who use the handkerchief or cross their legs when they are not expected to do so usually do not realize that they are breaking rules of etiquette and that they may be penalized. This chapter outlines some of the main problems that may be encountered by foreigners who meet the Japanese and speak to them either in English or in Japanese.

FOUR
RULES OF
LANGUAGE

The number of foreigners who decide to study the Japanese language is steadily growing and I hope that there will always be more and more of them. While a casual visitor to Japan can manage with speaking English, there is a great need for those who will build a more permanent base on which our understanding of the country can further develop. No doubt, knowledge of the Japanese language is a necessary prerequisite for such deeper understanding. However, the language is not merely important. It is also a tool of great refinement and beauty. In addition, the distance between Japanese and the language of most learners makes its study a process of discovery: discovery of new cultural forms as yet unencountered, and testifying to the enormous variation within human culture.

However, the distance between Japanese and other highly developed languages does not make it an easy target. Every teacher of Japanese has met people coming to learn the language in the belief that one or two hours per week over a year would make them speak and read it fluently. Of course, any amount of knowledge will be useful. However, it is necessary to realize that in order to speak and read Japanese with any degree of fluency, considerable effort is needed.

On the other hand, we should not imagine Japanese to be an "exotic" language. Human society, which has created languages, is basically the same throughout the world; and the brain, through which languages operate, as well as the larynx and the tongue—the ultimate tools for producing speech sounds—work across cultures in

153

the same way. All languages are basically made of the same material and Japanese *can* be conquered, as demonstrated by many foreigners over the last hundred years, and particularly the last decade.

JAPANESE AND OTHER LANGUAGES OF THE WORLD

What is the position of the Japanese language among other languages of the world? In linguistics, similarities and differences between languages can be measured on several scales, and the scales I propose to discuss here are (1) genetic relationship, (2) structural similarity, and (3) areal affinity.

Genetic Relationship

It is a well-known fact that languages can be classified into "language families" according to their historical origin. For instance, English, French, Russian, Albanian, Persian, Hindi, and many other languages have common parentage and belong to the "Indo-European Family." Hungarian, Finnish, Estonian, and other "Finno-Ugric" languages belong to another family, and a clear historical relationship can be established between Arabic, Hebrew, and other "Semitic" languages. Language families can be found in all parts of the world.

The Japanese linguist Shirō Hattori once remarked that probably few other languages have ever been subject to as many attempts to link them with other languages as Japanese. Most of these attempts lacked both the knowledge of facts and the rigor of a scientific method. It is only relatively recently that more reliable results have been obtained and have demonstrably connected Japanese with Korean and other languages of the East Asian Continent such as Mongol, Tungus, and the Turkic languages. There also remains the possibility of a common ancestry with some languages of the Pacific region, even if the ground here is more nebulous. On the other hand, more recent suggestions concerning the common origin of Japanese and Tamil need not be given serious hearing before more rigorous arguments are presented.

Genetically related languages which split relatively recently, perhaps two or three thousand years ago, usually retain a number of common words and gramatical features. The Germanic branch of the Indo-European family is a good example. Some languages of this family which split very recently, Swedish and Norwegian, for instance, are still mutually intelligible, while for other pairs of languages, such as English and German, the remaining common features of their lexicon are at least an important asset for a learner. However, in the case of languages which separated a long time ago, one must work hard to recognize their common origin. The vocabulary and grammar of such languages has changed too much. English and Hindi definitely belong to the same genetic family, but the originally identical words changed so much that their common parentage cannot be easily identified.

The same is true for Japanese and its Asian relatives. Time has erased their original similarity to such extent that it cannot be easily recognized. Recent advances in historical linguistics notwithstanding, for an average learner of Japanese the language is in practice still as isolated as it was fifty years ago.

Structural Similarity

Already in the nineteenth century linguistics firmly established that genetically related languages may possess completely different grammatical structures. For instance, within the Indo-European family contemporary English, Russian, and Hindi differ radically in their grammar. English uses predominantly grammatical procedures called analytical or *isolational*. Short isolated words with relatively few endings are arranged into sentences on the basis of the Subject-Verb-Object order (e.g., "John saw Paul"). On the other hand, in Russian (or Latin, for that matter), there is a large variety of endings, firmly integrated with word stems. Different stems attach different endings to express the same meaning. The morphology of the language is highly irregular. The word order is relatively free but the basic pattern is Subject-Verb-Object (i.e., the same as in English). Grammatical procedures of this type are usually referred to as *inflection*. However, the grammar of Hindi is different again. Hindi has longer words with a variety of endings and particles, and the word order rules place the Object before the Verb (one would say, in English paraphrase, "John Paul saw" in order to express the meaning of "John saw Paul."). This type of grammatical procedure has been called *agglutination*.

On the basis of what I shall describe later in this chapter, the reader will agree that the prevailing structural principle used in Japanese is agglutination. In Japanese, a variety of endings and particles are attached to words and there are few irregular forms. Like in Hindi, words are arranged into sentences in the Subject-Object-Verb order.

In Europe the principle of agglutination is charcteristic for Hungarian and Finnish and this has led some to assume that there might be a common ancestry with Japanese. However, the argument is faulty because structural similarity does not necessarily mean genetic relatedness. Agglutination as the most important grammatical principle can be found in many genetic families of languages throughout the world: in the Turkic languages; in India (both in the Indo-European and in the Dravidian language families); in Africa; among the indigenous American and Australian languages. The fact that agglutination is not prevalent in any of the major languages of international communication of the contemporary world is of course a matter of mere historical coincidence.

Areal Affinity

Languages can also be classified according to the lingistic area to which they belong. Languages spoken within the same area, particularly if they are all influenced by one or more culturally "strong" languages, usually share a large number of vocabulary items and possibly other features.

Within the European Area, for instance, a large number of words of Greek and Latin origin, as well as words borrowed from French or Italian and more recently English, are commonly shared. The Arabic Area spreads over a vast territory of the Islamic nations, from West Africa to Borneo. All languages of this area, whatever their genetic or structural type may have been, developed under the influence of Arabic.

Since the second half of the first millenium A.D., if not before, Japanese has been a member of the Far Eastern Area in which the Chinese language has figured as the principal source of influence. Japanese borrowed from Chinese a large number of lexical elements and, of course, the writing symbols (characters) which were necessary to write the lexicon down. The influence of China was pervasive in all areas of the use of language, literature, and thought. In this respect Japan was not alone: among others, Korea and Vietnam shared a similar history.

When Japan started modernizing its society and culture in the second half of the last century, it felt that this one-sided cultural and linguistic dependence on China would hold back its development. The necessity of alignment with the West was accepted, but was not achieved through a massive influx of Western words. The Japanese language of the second half of the nineteenth century took over from the West an enormous number of modern concepts, but these concepts were named with the help of lexical elements that had been borrowed from Chinese. For instance, the concept of ''an academic discipline'' was expressed in Japanese through a new word *kagaku*, composed of two elements borrowed from Chinese, *ka* (discipline) and *gaku* (learning); the new word was written with the characters which corresponded to these elements, 科 and 学.

Thus, with regard to the shapes of words, but not their meaning, Japanese basically remained a member of the Far Eastern linguistic area. However, it should be added that the ties between the languages of the area weakened when each of the languages of the area developed its modern vocabulary independently, although there was strong influence of Japanese, which modernized first, on Chinese and Korean. The differences further deepened when, after World War II, North Korea and subsequently, for some time, even South Korea, abandoned the use of characters, and when the shapes of characters were simplified in Japan and in China in different ways.

Apart from creating new vocabulary on the basis of Western meanings and formal elements borrowed from Chinese, Japanese also accepted a large number of foreign, mainly English, loanwords, the forms of which were assimilated to the sound structure of Japanese. The present-day relationship between Japanese and English was discussed in detail in the preceding chapter.

The fact that Japanese is genetically isolated from most of its partners, that it has a structure that is very different from all languages of international communication, and that it is not fully a member of the Anglophone area has exerted a strong influence on the competence of the Japanese to communicate in foreign languages. This also means that foreigners who are studying Japanese, unless they are members of the Far Eastern linguistic area, cannot receive much assistance in their study. For a German to learn Japanese is a task of a quite different order from learning English, French, Russian, or any other European language of the Indo-European family.

VARIETIES OF JAPANESE

Many of those who decide to study Japanese do not realize how vague the term "Japanese" is. There are many kinds of Japanese with which a learner normally comes into contact.

Standard Japanese

Standard Japanese (*hyōjungo*) is the name of the variety of Japanese which is taught in Japanese schools and used in writing throughout Japan. However, I shall explain below that the use of Standard Japanese in speaking is limited.

When examined in detail, Standard Japanese reveals a considerable degree of internal variation. Although basic grammar is shared, some styles include grammatical and vocabulary features that do not appear in other styles.

The hardest of all styles of Standard Japanese is that which can be called the "public style." It is used in law, administration, political writings, newspaper reporting, science and technology, and is characterized by a high percentage of difficult vocabulary composed of elements borrowed from Chinese. Some of its grammatical means derive from Classical Japanese. One can read novels for years without coming across the word *tenpu* (to be accompanied by). However, in order to read documents in the public style, words such as this are needed. Notice in particular that Japanese newspapers use a kind of this style. In many languages newspapers are relatively easy to read, but in Japanese they belong to the category of the most difficult texts. So do translations of many journalistic or scientific books.

A softer variety of the public style is employed in light journalism (weeklies and some other magazines), normally in the popularization of science, school textbooks (especially for junior high schools), and non-fiction literature for children. These texts are usually suitable for foreigners who have completed an advanced course and wish to commence independent reading.

The difficulty of the literary styles, used in prose, poetry, and literary translations, varies according to the period and the author. With the danger of overgeneralization we can say that Meiji literature is very difficult; Taishō literature, relatively easy; and the later Shōwa literature, including the literature of the postwar period, grows more difficult again. Fiction for children is not necessarily easy for foreign learners because it contains many items of special "children's vocabulary," and popular historical novels, with their special historical terminology and quasi-historical language in direct speech, are normally very difficult. In general, short novels usually contain more elaborate language than longer novels. Excerpts from the latter tend to be the easiest fiction to read.

Formal letters are written in an elaborate literary style, but the majority of private correspondence uses very simple language, probably the simplest of all varieties of written Japanese. Books on letter writing, available in large variety in all bookshops, usually contain only examples of the elaborate style, which is of little relevance for a learner of Japanese.

The use of the Standard language in speaking is limited to particular situations, such as T.V. and radio newscasting and announcements, public speaking (lectures and speeches), and formal face-to-face communication in public life; to public announcements in modes of transport and department stores; and to the speech of individuals in formal greetings (*aisatsu*). In all other situations in which the spoken language is used, in particular in private conversation, a variety of Japanese called Common Japanese (*kyōtsūgo*) is used.

Common Japanese and Regional Dialects

Common Japanese is a transitional form between the Standard and regional dialects, and exists in a number of varieties and gradations.

The Tokyo variety of Common Japanese is characterized by frequent contraction of some verbal forms (e.g., *tabete iru* → *tabeteru*, *tabete wa* → *tabecha*, *sō dewa* → *sō ja*), the use of some forms which do not exist in the Standard (e.g., *—tte*, *—kke*, and also *—chatta* for

—te shimatta), the addition of some case particles and some lexical features (e.g., *sake* [salmon] → *shake*, *ha* [leaves] → *happa*). The informal style of speaking is, strictly speaking, unavailable in the Standard and appears only in Common Japanese. Common Japanese of the Tokyo type is gaining currency in other areas of Japan and it is possible that it will become the variety used in speaking throughout the country.

In varieties of Common Japanese other than the Tokyo variety, some other features of the Standard are replaced by regional forms. For instance, the reduction of vowels (characteristic for the Standard and Tokyo Common Japanese) may be restricted, regional accent used, or individual grammatical and vocabulary items replaced by dialectal forms.

Foreign speakers of Japanese, unless their competence is very low, will normally be addressed in Common Japanese and will be expected to use one of its more ''Standard'' varieties in informal situations. As noted in Chapter III, they should be careful, when they travel to other areas of Japan, not to use forms that may be neutral in the area where they acquired the language, but may be labeled as dialectal in other areas.

The transition between Common Japanese and the regional dialects is as gradual as the transition from Standard to Common Japanese.

Japan has a large number of regional dialects, some of which, in their pure form, are incomprehensible to speakers from other parts of the country. This is paticularly true of some North-Eastern (Tōhoku) dialects spoken not very far away from Tokyo, and some dialects of the island of Kyūshū. Dialects of the Ryūkyū islands are very distant from all other Japanese dialects and are totally incomprehensible, even when spoken very slowly. On the other hand, the difference between the Tokyo speech and the Kansai dialects (spoken in and around Kyoto and Osaka) is relatively small. In any case, dialectal diversity does not cause major practical problems, because virtually all Japanese can use a variety of Common Japanese when speaking with people who do not know their regional dialect.

In general, we can say that the more formal a situation is, the more Standard-like the language is that is used; on the contrary, the more informal the situation, the larger the number of regional characteristics that are used in the language of the speakers, especially if they all come from the same region. In a radio interview, Mr. Yoshida may use the Standard language as such. When speaking with the announcer after the interview, he is likely to include in his speech features of the Common language of his area, and the number of such features will increase when he goes to lunch with his colleagues. As a matter of fact, if they are all speakers of the same dialect, the language used may become a pure regional dialect. In other than urban areas the dialect is used widely, not only in informal communication within families and among friends, but even in shops and in public life. Tokyo, too, has its regional dialect, though relatively weak, but some speakers in Tokyo, mainly middle-class people, avoid many of the clearly dialectal features. The middle-class speech is referred to as Yamanote speech, while the dialectally colored speech is called the Shitamachi (Downtown) dialect.

Linguistic features of Common Japanese and the regional dialects also appear in print. Most Japanese magazines contain a transcript of a round-table discussion (*zadankai*) which is usually presented in Japanese oscillating between the Standard and the Common language. The cartoon story books (*manga*), direct speech in fiction, and most theatre plays employ a variety of Common Japanese of the Tokyo type, except when the author wants to add a regional flavor. In that case, dialectal features are introduced. However, in most instances, the "dialect" used in literature consists of features taken from various dialects and does not portray any particular variety of Japanese.

Spoken and Written Japanese

From what has been said so far the reader will understand that there is a considerable distance between the language that is spoken and the language that is used in written documents. The written language is the more difficult variety, but it cannot be skipped by learners who intend to use their knowledge for any serious purpose. Students who do not read the newspapers cannot normally understand the language of newsreading on the radio and television and cannot converse about politics or serious social issues. Japanese is a language that is strongly dependent on its written form, not merely for reading the literature, but for any practical purpose. This is often a source of misunderstanding between native speakers of Japanese (who can "hear" that a foreign speaker cannot read and write) and foreign speakers who believe that after having gone through an elementary course of Japanese and mastering *kana* and a few hunderd characters are ready to join Japanese networks.

Classical Japanese

Classical Japanese is a set of varieties that cannot be omitted from any survey of contemporary Japanese. They are not simply a matter of history; some of the varieties are still used in contemporary cultural and social life.

The first extensive texts written in Japanese, mostly *tanka* (31-syllable poems), date back to the eighth century. At the beginning of the eleventh century, in the Heian period, Japanese already possessed a literature of great variety and lasting literary values. The *Tale of Genji,* completed in this period, is one of the classics of world literature.

New styles were added later as the historical novel, the Noh drama, Kabuki, haiku, and the prose of the Tokugawa period developed. The common feature of the language of all this literature is that though occasionally it may have come close to the spoken language of its period, its basic component always remained Heian grammar and vocabulary. It was in the Meiji period that the Colloquial Standard, basically identical with the contemporary Standard, first developed on the basis of the spoken language of Tokyo. However, the acceptance of this Colloquial Standard was only gradual. It first won in fiction, then in other literature and in the newspapers. However, the language of administration and law was, until after World War II, the Classical Standard, a variety of Classical Japanese. This language retained many words of the classical styles and its grammar was totally different from the grammar of the modern spoken language.

In contemporary Japan, the Classical Standard still survives in practical communication as the language of legal codes promulgated before 1946. For instance the Commercial Code is written in this language, and current amendments are still drafted in the same style. Classical Japanese is also the language of the traditional arts. Some of the contemporary *tanka* and haiku poetry is still composed in this language and traditional plays are performed in Classical Japanese, even if sometimes adapted for modern audiences.

Classical Japanese is of course taught in schools and a considerable reading competence is achieved by better students. Yet, classical literature, when read for other than study purposes, is normally read in modern translation. (The Commercial Code and other similar codes are also available in translation into the contemporary Standard language.)

Foreigner Talk and Textbook Japanese

In all languages of the world, foreign speakers who have not achieved semi-native competence are usually addressed in a simplified variety of language called in linguistics Foreigner Talk. In its weak form it implies only a slow tempo of speech, careful pronunciation, and simplification of content and vocabulary. In an extreme case an adult may be addressed with sentences such as "Soup yummy?"

Japanese is no exception in this respect. Foreigners who do not possess a semi-native competence must accept that the Japanese used toward them will be more or less a weaker or a stronger variety of Foreigner Talk. For instance, few honorifics may be used, pronouns (*watashi* "I," *anata* "you") may appear with increased frequency, English words may replace Japanese words, and conversation topics may be simplified. The style of speech will be careful and slow and Standard forms may appear instead of forms of Common Japanese.

The language most teachers of Japanese use with foreigners in classrooms is necessarily a variety of Foreigner Talk. So is the language of textbooks. Introductory textbooks of Japanese usually present a simplified neutral form of the Standard language. On one hand, this is not the language employed in daily conversation in Tokyo. Such language, as mentioned above, is Common Japanese, not the Standard. Learners, after leaving their classrooms, are usually shocked by the contrast between formal and informal speech and by the large number of grammatical forms encountered in conversation that they had never heard of in the classroom. On the other hand, they are also surprised by the fact that in order to read normal written texts, in particular in the "public style" (newspapers, academic texts, tect.) they need not only additional characters but also additional grammar, phraseology, and vocabulary in amounts they had never expected.

The existence of Foreigner Talk and Textbook Japanese certainly hides from the learner the true shape of the Japanese language. However, it is possible to argue that it also makes his first steps in the language easier, and so long as the learner does not take it for the real and ultimate Japanese, Foreigner Japanese can assist him in the acquisition of the language.

JAPANESE: A BRIEF OUTLINE

What are the main characteristic features of the Japanese language? The answer will differ depending on the basis of comparison we adopt. In the following survey, I shall take the point of view of English, not because English would be the natural yardstick to measure other languages, but because I assume that readers of this book are more familiar with the structure of English than that of any other single language. This survey will attempt to employ an idiom that is ''conservative'' from the point of view of linguistics, but which should be easily comprehensible even to a complete layman.

Basic Sounds

Compared with English, the number of basic sounds of Japanese is small. There are:

(a) 5 short vowels: a   i   u   e   o

(b) 17 basic consonants: k   t   s   sh   p
                             g   d   z   j   b
                             h   r   ch   w   y*
                                 n   m

> *For instance, as in *yama* (mountain); note that when used after a consonant (as in *kyō* [today]) the letter *y* indicates a softening of the preceding consonant and is not a full consonant itself.

(c) the nasal *n*, which occurs only at the end of a syllable as in

hon (book) or *densha* (train); in *kana* there is a special symbol
for this sound, but in romanization it is normally represented
as n; the pronunciation is mostly the same as for a nasalized
vowel.

Only the nasal *n* is somehow out of the ordinary. All other basic
sounds are very common and appear in many languages of the
world. Rules for the prounciation of sounds in the above list cannot
be given here. In the above list the sounds of Japanese are represented
in one of the most widely used systems of romanization, the Revised
Hepburn system. Let me only note that in this system the vocalic
symbols are read in principle as in Italian, while the consonantal
symbols have the same value as in English. Of course, the pronunciation of some of them differs from the pronunciation of sounds that
are written with the same letter in Italian or English. Perhaps the
most representative example is the sound of the letter *r*, which is difficult to pronounce for many foreigners.

On the whole, the system of Japanese vowels and consonants as
given above may look quite simple. However, when these basic
sounds combine into syllables and syllables into words, certain adaptive changes take place and a few new "secondary" sounds appear.
So, for instance, *h* + *u* gives *fu* (with a new consonant *f*), *t* + *u*
gives *tsu* (with a new consonant *ts*), and the consonant *g* can be
nasalized and give as ŋ under certain conditions.

The most radical of these changes is the full or partial dropping
("reduction" or "devoicing") of vowels in certain positions. The
vowels *i* and *u* are most strongly affected. For instance, the famous
dish sukiyaki is pronounced *s'kiyaki* in Japanese, except in a very
slow "spelling pronunciation." "Prime Minister Kishi" becomes,
in the cased of full reduction, *K'sh'sh'shō* (Kishi-*shushō*) and when
there was a Prime Minister of this name, even Japanese listeners complained that they could not catch on the radio who the announcer
was speaking about. Learners of Japanese should remember that the
reduction of vowels is a feature that differentiates Standard Japanese
from the dialects and must, therefore, be given proper attention.

As a consequence of these adaptive changes, spoken Japanese has a
less monotonous sound structure than we might expect. Although
in theory each syllable has exactly the same duration, in practice their
length differs a great deal, depending on the degree of reduction, the
position of the syllable in the word, and accentuation. For instance,

in casual prounciation the name of the famous author Akutagawa may sound something like [a]ktāŋã[a] with the vowel *u* completely reduced, the consonant *g* pronounced as a nasal, the second and third vowel also weakly nasalized, the consonant *w* almost fully reduced, and both the first and the last vowels considerably weakened.

Sequences of Vowels and Consonants

One characteristic feature of sound sequences in Japanese is that several vowels often follow each other (e.g., *aoi* [blue]). Whole sentences, though rarely of notable content, can be constructed of vowels only. For instance *O o ōō* (Let's cover the tail) consists of two short *o*'s and two long *o*'s.

All vowels can be either short or long. In more careful pronunciation, the long vowels can be pronounced as a sequence of the same vowel (e.g., *ō* as *oo*), and this is also how they are often romanized. The pronunciation of each such long (double) vowel takes nearly twice the time of the corresponding short sound. This is also true about consonants that can be long (double) and are in this case normally romanized as a repetition of the same sound: kk, tt, ss, etc. Only the double (long) ch is romanized irregularly as tch. The double (long) consonants are pronounced as one sound, except that the tongue is held in the middle of the consonants twice as long as in the case of the short consonant (much as in the Italian pronunciation of them).

Many words are distinguished in this way, for instance *to* ''door'' and *tō* ''ten''; *kata* ''shoulder'' and *katta* ''have won.'' Wrong pronunciation can easily lead to misunderstanding. If you want to say that he is an Australian, you must say *gōshūjin*. *Goshujin*, with short vowels, means ''husband.'' *Ite kudasai* means ''stay here'' while *itte kudasai* means ''go away.'' On a certain occasion, I noticed that a student of mine was consistently saying *otōsan no otōsan* ''father's father'' instead of *ojiisan* ''grandfather.'' His explanation was that he could not pronounce the long (double) vowel in *ojiisan* long enough, and had the experience of being misunderstood. *Ojisan* with a single (short) vowel *i* means ''uncle.''

Apart from double (long) consonants, the sound *n* (which is closer to a nasal vowel than to a consonant) and *y* (which is more a graphical symbol of softening of the preceding consonant, or at most a semi-vowel), two consonants can never follow each other; neither can a consonant (except for the nasal *n*, which is closer to a vowel) appear at the end of a word. This is a useful guide for identifying Japanese names. For example, Mr. Masubda cannot be a Japanese because the name contains the sequence bd. Of course it should be borne in mind that this rule only applies to the written language. As mentioned above, in spoken Japanese vowels are often reduced and this results in the appearance of a number of consonantal clusters.

The Accent

There are many stories about misunderstanding due to the Japanese accent. For instance, a man from the country asked in a restaurant for *káki* (oysters; accent on first vowel), and was offered a serving of *kaki* (persimmons; no accent) instead. A girl complained about her boyfriend who, she believed, promised to take her to see *Fúji* (Mt. Fuji; accent on first syllable), but it turned out that he meant *fuji* (wistaria; no accent) in the local park. Such misunderstandings, real or assumed, result from dialectal difference in accentuation. The accent of individual words differs in many dialects and it is not easy, for native speakers of the dialects, to acquire the Standard accent, which is the accent of the Tokyo area. There are many pairs of words distinguished only through the accent. For example, in the Standard pronunciation *ippai* means "a lot," while *íppai* means "one cup." *Hashí* means "a bridge," while *háshi* means "chopsticks." In other dialects the pronunciation is sometimes exactly the opposite of the Standard pattern.

The Japanese system of accentuation differs considerably from English stress. Sometimes it is referred to as a "pitch accent" but we should realize that it has nothing to do either with singing or with the Chinese tones. If it is to be compared with the accentuation of any other language, then the Swedish or Serbo-Croatian accent could be given as the closest analogies.

Foreign learners of Japanese should not be unduly worried that mistakes in the accent will cause frequent misunderstandings of the beginners' speech. As a matter of fact, such misunderstandings are very rare. However, the accent is important for a different reason: it helps to identify the boundaries between words and to preserve the audibility of all syllables within a long word. Foreigners who wish to be clearly understood must acquire at least the basic rules of Japanese accentuation. And this is not difficult to achieve.

Norms of Pronunciation in Contact Situations

As long as foreigners struggle with their basic Japanese sentence patterns and the basic vocabulary, native speakers of Japanese will not be bothered about their accent. However, as the competence of foreign speakers improves, stricter criteria are applied. This phenomenon has already been referred to above. You will find that the Japanese will not merely think that you said something else, but many refuse to understand quite common words which you pronounced with the wrong accent. Requirements placed on foreign speaker's pronunciation are often stricter than in the case of native speakers of Japanese. Again, this is a general feature of many languages and is not limited to Japanese.

Foreign speakers of Japanese are expected to approximate those norms of pronunciation that native speakers value most: the norms of the Standard language. The accent is included but it is not merely the accent. Native speakers who themselves do not adhere to the norm will encourage you to nasalize the consonant *g* in all cases in which, according to the conservative norm, it can be nasalized. Many speakers of Japanese from other than the Tokyo area reduce the vowels *u* and *i* differently: their usage may not be noted as incorrect but yours may. These are facts of life which have to be accepted.

JAPANESE GRAMMAR

Some Basic Features

In English some words are inflected (dog → dogs, bark → barked, etc.) but in general such inflections are scarce. Relations between words are expressed by prepositions (of, to, from, etc.) or by word order (John saw Joan, Joan saw John). The basic word order in English is Subject-Verb-Object. Auxiliaries, like prepositions, or the verbs to be, shall, etc., precede the word to which they belong (*to* John, I *am* eating a cake, he *will* see). On the other hand, relative clauses follow the noun to which they are attached (I saw the man *who wasn't there*).

The variety of Japanese that we shall describe in the present section of this chapter is what was called above "Textbook Japanese." Grammatically, it overlaps in all details discussed here with Standard Japanese. Of course, the grammar of Common Japanese, the language used in daily conversation, is somewhat different.

In Japanese, verbs and adjectives take a variety of endings, suffixes, and auxiliary words. Look at some of the possible changes in some words: *taberu* (to eat) → *tabeta, tabereba, tabemasu, tabemashitara, tabete mo, taberu no de*; or *takai* (high) → *takaku, takakatta, takakereba, takai no de, takai deshō, . . .*). These changes of the form of the words mostly serve the same purpose as the English auxiliaries. Nouns take one or more particles: *inu* (dog) → *inu wa, inu made, inu no de mo*, etc., working roughly like English prepositions or word order. For instance,

Takahashi-san wa Jōn o mimashita. (Mr. Takahashi saw Joan).

The following notes will help the reader to understand the structure of the sentence:

1. The personal name Takahashi is here followed by the suffix *-san* which means "Mr./Mrs./Miss".

2. In this sentence the particle *wa* indicates that the preceding word is the "subject" of the sentence.

3. *Jōn* is the Japanese pronunciation of Joan.

4. The particle *o* indicates that the preceding word is the grammatical "object" of the verb.

5. *Mimashita* is the polite past tense form of the verb *miru* (to see). The form consists of the stem *mi-* (to see), the polite ending *-mash-*, a connecting vowel *-i-*, and the past tense ending *-ta*.

As long as the same particles are used after nouns, the order of the nouns in the sentence can change, without a resulting change in meaning. The above sentence can also appear in the form *Jōn o Takahashi-san wa mimashita*. (The new sentence can of course only appear in contexts different from the contexts of the original sentence. This matter will not be discussed here.)

In romanization, a space is usually left before each particle, but in Japanese writing no spaces are normally used between elements of a sentence, and in speech all particles are pronounced together with their noun as one long word.

On the basis of the sentence we can now identify the first two grammatical hurdles for a learner of Japanese.

Problem 1: Unlike in English, a stem of a word or a word is followed by one or more endings, suffixes, or particles.

This makes Japanese difficult for speakers of languages that employ few or no such grammatical elements. Indeed, native speakers of English sometimes omit particles after nouns. However, the task of the learner is alleviated by the fact that except for some verbal forms, the additions of these endings, suffixes, and particles follows regular patterns. There are very few irregular verbs and no differences of "paradigms" such as in the Russian or Latin declensions.

Problem 2: Japanese words, with all their endings, suffixes, and particles, are considerably longer units than words in English.

When pronouncing these words an attempt must be made not to cut them into shorter segments. Because some particles are preceded by a space in romanization, many learners who start learning Japanese from romanized texts put a brief pause before them, pronouncing, for instance *Takahashi*-pause-*san*-pause-*wa*. . . However, such pronunciation is utterly incorrect and can lead to a complete loss of comprehensibility.

Further, although under particular contextual conditions the order of nouns within a sentence can change relatively easily, the basic word order in Japanese is Subject-Object-Verb. Auxiliaries, like particles, follow the word to which they belong. For instance, *Boku wa furūto o naratte imasu* (I am learning [how to play] the flute). Note that in this sentence,

1. The word *boku* "I" (used by male speakers in informal situations) is followed by the particle *wa*, which in this sentence marks the subject;
2. *Furūto* is the Japanese pronunciation of flute, and is followed by the "object" particle *o* (in English the object has no special marking, it is simply the noun placed *after* the verb); and
3. *Naratte* is a gerundive form of the verb *narau* (to study, to learn), which together with the auxiliary *imasu* corresponds roughly to the English "am/is/are learning"; note that the form of the verb

would be the same if the subject was "he," "she," or "they"; unlike the English or the French or Latin verb, to be, the verbal form does not change in dependence on the subject.

Adjectives and relative clauses precede their nouns. Observe, for instance, the phrase *akai bōshi* (a red hat), where *akai* means "red" and *bōshi* "hat," or *soko ni inakatta hito* (the man who wasn't there) where *soko* is "that place, there," *ni* is a particle that mostly corresponds to the English preposition in/at/to (*soko ni* being literally "at that place"), and *inakatta* is the past tense of *inai* "is not"; the whole phrase means "wasn't there" and it stands before the noun *hito* "a/the man." Notice that the English relative pronoun "who" is not expressed in Japanese.

On the basis of the last three examples we can go on to formulate Problem 3.

Problem 3: The order of words and clauses is frequently the reverse of the English order.

Few, if any learners find this initial obstacle insurmountable, but they must often exert some effort to overcome it. I have seen, on many occasions, how foreigners who were using interpreters stopped in the middle of an English sentence, in order to make it easier for the interpreter to translate. As a result, the interpreter could not proceed at all, because he was waiting for the second part of the sentence to begin with.

Problem 4: Distinctions commonly made in English are not made in Japanese, while some distinctions made in Japanese are not encountered in English.

As mentioned above, the Japanese verb does not distinguish between (I) am, (s/he) is, or (they) are. The form of the verb is the same whatever the subject may be. Moreover, the pronoun (I, she, he, you, they), obligatory in English, is not used in Japanese unless it cannot be retrieved from the context or other cues. It can take some time for a foreigner to become convinced that the English I, you, etc. are often there for no other reason than that they are required by the rules of English grammar, and that a Japanese sentence will be perfectly well understood even if the Japanese equivalent of the English pronoun is dropped. On the other hand, when the pronoun is being used, the speaker must normally select in Japanese one of a number of words, thus using distinctions that are not made in

English. For instance, I normally use *boku* "I" with my wife, *watashi* "I" with out-group addressees, *watakushi* "I" in a formal situation, and I can also occasionally use *ore*, or *watakushime*, etc. as a joke. Foreigners who acquired Japanese mainly in informal situations may find it particularly difficult to differentiate between the informal *boku*, and more formal *watashi*.

A similar case occurs with the plural. Only personal pronouns require special plural forms in Japanese: *watashi* "I" → *watashitachi* "we" or its equivalent. For nouns denoting persons, and to a smaller extent animals, a plural form is optional; for nouns denoting objects no plural form exists at all. Normally this causes no communication problems, because in an extreme case, when a misunderstanding could arise, the speaker can always use a numeral to specify how many people, animals, or objects are meant. A rare, actually observed case of misunderstanding occurred in a Japanese restaurant. A Japanese couple with a little boy left after finishing their dinner; however, in a few minutes, the boy returned, picked up a glove that was on the chair where his mother had sat and ran out, only to come back in seconds, to collect the second glove, which had fallen under the chair. Should his mother have given him instructions in English, she would have differentiated between "glove" and "gloves." However, in Japanese the key word was *tebukuro* "glove, gloves," which like any other object noun does not make a distinction between the singular and the plural. Since the boy could only see one glove, he assumed that his mother meant the singular "glove" when she sent him to collect it, and only on delivering it was told that both gloves had been left in the restaurant.

Among the distinctions that are not made in English but are obligatory in Japanese is the difference between two types of subjects: those which require the particle *wa*, and those which require the particle *ga*. The distinction is rather complicated and cannot be discussed here in detail; however, I shall give an example of two of the many usages involved. In the sentence *Koitsu wa dorobō da* "This guy is a thief." Analyzing this sentence gives the following: *koitsu* (this guy); *dorobō* (thief); *da* (an informal copula meaning "is"); the particle *wa* after *koitsu* implies either a contrast (i.e., this guy is a *thief*, but not a murderer, as someone else might be) or simply a subject.

On the other hand, let's consider *Koitsu ga dorobō da* "This guy is a thief." With the particle *ga* after *koitsu*, this sentence means something like "It is *this* guy who is a thief," with an emphasis on "*this* guy." In the communication process, it is of course quite important to know when a contrast is implied and when a word is emphasized. Hence, correct usage of the two particles is not merely a matter of correctness but also of communicative efficiency.

I shall add that at the intermediate stage of the study of Japanese another hurdle appears: the length of sentences. Japanese, written or conversational, uses quite long and sometimes quite complicated sentences. The ability of foreign speakers to pass over from a sequence of short sentences to the usual Japanese sentential structure marks the final transition from the intermediate to the advanced level of competence.

Honorifics

Another example of distinctions that are virtually absent in English but must be made in Japanese are honorific distinctions. In Japanese, speakers must use different verbal (and some other) forms depending on to whom and about whom they are speaking. For instance, even when asking a simple question such as "Will she go?," at least four different situations must be distinguished:

1. When speaking *to* an in-group person (e.g., the speaker's brother, a close friend) *about* the speaker's classmate (i.e., a junior) the verb will be *iku*.

2. When still speaking *to* an in-group person but *about* your teacher's wife who happens to be present (i.e., a senior), the verb will change to *irassharu*.

3. When speaking *to* a visitor (out-group) *about* one's classmate, the verb will be *ikimasu*.

4. When speaking *to* a visitor (teacher) *about* the visitor's wife, the verb must be *irasshaimasu*.

You can easily see that the difference between speaking to in-group and out-group participants is in attaching the ending *-masu*, (after which the question particle *ka* is normally used). The difference between speaking about juniors and seniors relies on the use of a different verb: *iku* in the former case, and the honorific verb *irassharu* in the latter. These four examples show the most important dimensions of the Japanese honorific system. Of course, when we speak in other situations and use different verbs, the situation will change and may become more complicated. Also, there is another level of speech that is usually called the very polite (*gozaimasu* or deferential) style and in which foreigners will sometimes be addressed, though they may not be obliged to use it.

No similar distinctions are made in English, but all other European languages and many non-European languages make distinction between in-group and out-group and/or junior and senior participants. For instance in French, in-group participants are addressed with *tu* (you), while with out-group participants the more honorific pronouns *vous* must be used.

As already mentioned, Japanese pronouns, though not very frequently used, show considerable variation and some of the distinctions are honorific.

In the case of some nouns, a twofold distinction exists, but by far not all nouns have both forms. There is a basic form and an honorific form which prefixes *o-* (or for some words *go-*) to the basic form. For instance, "nose" is *hana* or *o-hana*, "book" is *hon* or *go-hon*. The prefixed form can be used about a senior's possession, for example, when speaking to a senior about his nose or book, one can say *o-hana,* or *go-hon.* However, a more important use of the prefixed forms is in "soft speech," that is, speech of women and children or speech directed to women and children. For instance a mother speaking to her child will say *o-hana* when speaking to the child about his nose, and *go-hon* when speaking to him about the book he is playing with. The honorific prefixation is not available for some nouns at all. On the other hand, with some nouns the prefix is used so frequently that the basic form alone gives a rather harsh impression (e.g., *kane* as against *o-kane* "money"), and in the case of some nouns the form without the suffix is very rare or non-existent (e.g., *o-cha* "tea"). Some honorific forms of verbs also convey the same meaning of "softness."

Foreigners and Japanese Honorifics

The honorific system is of course one of the major parts of the Japanese grammatical system that must be studied if a foreign speaker wishes to correctly communicate about his or her attitudes, intentions, and personality. Though complicated, the system is not as difficult as some foreigners believe. Unfortunately, some learners have a negative attitude about its acquisition based on the incorrect assumption that when using honorifics the speaker is establishing relations of superiority and inferiority, flattering some addressees and insulting others. Nothing of the sort is involved. Although honorifics can sometimes be employed in this way among native speakers, their application by foreigners usually implies nothing else than the normal amount of consideration and politeness, required in any community, and normally practiced by anyone. Some of those who do not wish to use honorifics do not hesitate to be polite in their native language at all. They address their teachers with their titles and last name, for example, Dr. Miller or Professor So-and-So, although they are being addressed with their first name, and this irreciprocal arrangement does not appear to them to violate their sense of equality and justice. The use of Japanese honorifics does not in fact imply more than the irreciprocal address does in English.

Foreigners with a different history of acquiring the language may have different problems. For instance, former high-school exchange students who acquired their Japanese mainly from their school friends and the families they lived with in Japan often show considerable fluency in basic communicative in-group situations while being unable to handle communication with out-group participants. They must learn how to use the out-group honorific forms and how to use honorific forms about senior people referred to in their speech. On the other hand, students who studied Japanese in language courses offered overseas may have acquired quite a number of honorific forms from reading Japanese literature and may be faced with the need to rather restrict their usage. The avoidance of honorifics is an important communicative technique for both native speakers and advanced foreign learners. If speakers underuse honorifics they are being impolite. However, if they overuse honorifics, they create too much communicative distance and it may be difficult for them to establish close informal relationship with native speakers.

One final note. The Japanese term for honorifics is *keigo*, but the word tends to denote, for average speakers of Japanese, the high level of honorifics used in the very polite (deferential or *gozaimasu*) style. This accounts for misunderstandings when honorifics are discussed.

Foreign speakers are interested in the normal everyday range of honorific expressions, but if they use the word *keigo*, their Japanese partners may assume that they are referring to the high honorifics and may feel that this certainly is something that a foreign student who has hardly reached the intermediate stage of competence should not be interested in.

Male and Female Language

There are many differences between the ways male and female speakers communicate in any language. These differences concern the switch-on rules, the participant rules, content rules, channel (non-verbal communication) rules, and many others. However, what is typical for Japanese (though not for Japanese alone) is the fact that the difference also affects the grammar of the language. Of course, pronouns are used differently, but the specific feature is in the use of what is called the "sentence final particles."

Sentence final particles are in the informal styles of Japanese almost obligatory and communicate, very broadly speaking, the attitude of the speaker. For instance, as an answer to the question *Iku?* "Will you go?" male speakers can also answer simply *Iku* (with no final particle), but normally they will attach a final particle: *Iku yo* (with the particle *yo*), *Iku zo* (with the particle *zo*) or similar. However, a female speaker will respond differently: *Iku, Iku wa, Iku no, Iku wa yo,* or *Iku no yo* are the most usual alternatives. The differences in meaning between these expressions are difficult to translate. Note that male and female speakers use different particles, and that if the same particle is used, it connects differently with the preceding word. For instance, when the particle *ne* "isn't it" is attached to nouns, a male speaker says *Tōkyō da ne* "It's Tokyo, isn't it," while a female speaker says *Tōkyō ne* (without the particle *da* in between).

Young girls often apply the male usage when they communicate among themselves, but switch over to the more feminine usage when their speech is monitored. The rules are still distinct. Former female exchange students usually have a problem here, because they often have not acquired the "proper" female final particles. On the other hand, if a male adult foreigner says *Iku wa*, everyone will be amused because this will be taken to mean that he learned the phrase from a female speaker, perhaps a bar hostess.

Parts of Speech

Even a brief survey of Japanese grammar would remain incomplete without mentioning the main parts of speech.

Nouns, in Japanese, take particles, which are pronounced together with the noun, even if in romanization they are spelled separately. Particles can be divided into case particles, conjunctive particles, and limiting particles. Case particles define the relationship between words in the sentence, for example *ga* means the subject, *o* the direct object, *no* the modifier, etc. Conjunctive particles connect several nouns which have the same relationship to other words, as, for example, in *Takashi to Ryōzō ni aimashita* "We met Takashi and Ryōzō," where the particle *to* is used to connect two nouns (Takashi and Ryōzō) both of which stand in the same relationship to the verb. The relationship is a relationship of a direct object and is indicated in the sentence by the use of the particle *ni* after the second of the two nouns. The third category, the limiting particles, includes such particles as *wa*, which as we know, can be used among other things for contrast. Combinations of various particles are possible, as for example, in *o-cha no o demo* "even that of tea," where the modifier case particle *no* is followed by the object particle *o* and finally the limiting particle *demo* "even" is used.

Pronouns in Japanese behave mostly like nouns. They have no special grammatical features of their own, except for the fact, mentioned above, that the plural of pronouns is obligatory. *Watashi* means "I," never "we." In order to say "we" the speaker must say *watashitachi*. Remember that there is no really polite second person pronoun (you). The word *anata* must not be used toward seniors. Names with *-san* or titles are employed instead.

The copula (the word which expresses that A *is* B) is attached to the noun as a particle. The copula is inflected in a way similar to the inflection of the verb. "It is a lie" is *uso da*; "it was a lie" is *uso datta*; "if it were a lie" is *uso dattara*; etc. (Note that the word "it" is not used in Japanese.)

Verbs can be divided into two classes that take suffixes and endings somewhat differently: vocalic verbs and consonantal verbs. *Taberu* (to eat) is an example of the former; *yomu* (to read), of the latter. Various suffixes can modify the verbal stem before endings are attached. The most common modifications are the passive, the causative, the polite form (*-mas-*), and the desiderative. The endings are the present/future ending, the past tense ending (*-ta/-da*), the gerundive ending (*-te/-da*), the conditional endings (*-ba* and *-tara/-dara*), the presumptive (*-ō*), the past presumptive, and the alternative (*-tari/-dari*). The stem of a verb can also be used independently in a way similar to the gerundive or as a noun. A number of auxiliary verbs, nouns, or suffixes can be added to the basic verbal form, and such elements can again be followed by suffixes, endings, and particles, with the final particle coming last. All these additions to the basic verb stem are likely to be pronounced as one long verb.

A special type of verbs are verbs formed by adding the auxiliary verb *suru* (to do) to a noun. Many verbs belong to this type, for example, *benkyō suru* (to study), *ryokō suru* (to travel), etc.

While in most Indo-European languages adjectives are close to nouns, in Japanese some adjectives are close to verbs, while others behave more or less as nouns. In the case of the former type, to say "He is quick" no copula is needed, we just say *hayai* ([he is] quick). To say "He was quick" we change the ending of the adjective to *hayakatta*, as if we said in English "[he] quicked." So this type of adjective inflects in very much the same way as the verb or the copula. The adjectives which are close to verbs end in *-i*. The other type of adjectives, which are closer to nouns, have no endings. They attach the copula to express the past tense and other forms, as in, for example, *kirei datta* (it was beautiful). When they modify nouns, these adjectives use the particle *na*: *kirei na machi* (a beautiful town).

Adverbs can be formed from adjectives by changing the ending: *hayai* (quick) → *hayaku* (quickly); *kirei na* (beautiful) → *kirei ni* (beautifully), but there are of course many adverbs not derived from adjectives. Numerals behave in Japanese mostly in the same way as adverbs.

Numerals are difficult to use in most languages but this is particularly true about Japanese. There are basically two types of numerals: original Japanese numerals and numerals borrowed from Classical Chinese. The user must know when to use each of these two types and how to combine numerals with "counting suffixes," which are required for some objects. For instance, instead of "two books" one says "two-volume books," where the counting suffix corresponds to the word "volume." There are many irregular changes and the accentuation of numerals is also very difficult. Like in Chinese and other East Asian languages Japanese has a special word for 10,000. So, 25,000 is "two ten-thousands and five thousands" and 1,000,000 is "one hundred ten-thousands." This difference requires some effort when large numbers are used, not merely for foreigners, but also. for the Japanese when they use English.

There are other less frequently used parts of speech in Japanese, but the scope of this book does not allow us to describe each of them individually.

VOCABULARY

Types of Vocabulary

Japanese has a refined and extensive vocabulary that can express all possible shades of meaning necessary for contemporary intellectual and material life. On the basis of its origin, this vocabulary can be classified into three distinct groups.

1. *J-words.* These words derive from the original, native Japanese vocabulary. Words such as *ki* "a tree," *hashi* "a bridge," *inochi* "life," *yaoya* "greengrocer's," *natsuyasumi* "summer vacation," *yomu* "to read," *muzukashii* "difficult," *sugu* "immediately," and thousands of others belong to this category. These J-words represent the most neutral, basic vocabulary of Japanese.

2. *SJ-words.* Words which belong to this group are composed of elements borrowed together with characters from Chinese during the second half of the first millenium A.D. Their pronunciation and sometimes also their meaning have, however, diverged from Chinese so radically that when pronounced they cannot be recognized as originally Chinese elements.

Some of these Sino-Japanese elements are words on their own (e.g., *hon* "a book," *niku* "meat"), but mostly two or more combine to form one word. Much of this compounding was done in the

Meiji era, and some of the resulting words, mostly scientific and technical terms, were borrowed back into modern Chinese. Examples of the compounds are *gaku* + *kō* → *gakkō* "school," or *byō* + *ri* + *gaku* → *byōrigaku* "pathology." Though some of the SJ-compounds are stylistically neutral, many are marked as "stiff" or "bookish." In English, words borrowed from Latin or Greek resemble this category to a considerable extent.

3. *L-words.* These words are relatively recent loans from languages other than Chinese, with an especially intensive inflow from English. For instance, *beru* "a bell," *purojekuto* "a project," *erebētā* "an elevator." Quite a few elements have been combined to form new words which do not exist in the same form in the language of origin (e.g., *miruku tī* "tea with milk"). Of course, English too, apart from older borrowings, has a substantial number of new loanwords, mainly from French (e.g., ballet, lingerie, ennui, etc.), but also from other languages, including Japanese (e.g., judo, ikebana, sukiyaki, etc.).

It was mentioned in Chapter Three that many new words are introduced from English into Japanese on an ad hoc and temporary basis. One reasons for this is that a foreign word carries with it the atmosphere of a most recent and fashionable object or idea. However, there are also linguistic reasons, the most important being that the formation of new words from J- or SJ- elements has stagnated for some time and a foreign loan is the easiest way to create a new term that sounds like a special term, and is neither too long, nor too bookish. Some of the newly introduced words gain a permanent status in the language, others disappear and are replaced by other words. It is also important to realize that many loan words from English are only used in conversation or informal styles of writing and are often replaced by synonymous SJ-words in formal written language.

The presence of an extensive English vocabulary in Japanese creates of course very favorable conditions for foreign speakers. When a Japanese word is not known, foreign speakers can try the corresponding English word and search for the correct Japanese equivalent. This method is successful not merely in the case of scientific and difficult technical terminologies but also in the case of a car repairman or a hardware store. In the course of such searches, all

English words should of course be pronounced in the accepted Japanese pronunciation of English.

In contemporary Japanese, these three groups of words are relatively strictly differentiated: each group is marked by a number of phonetic and grammatical features, and when compounds are formed, normally only elements from the same group combine. Of course, there is a certain percentage of "mixed words."

The Use of Words

Throughout the older history of the Japanese language the J-words were dominant, except in those literary styles, such as the pre-Meiji historical novel, which developed under the strong influence of Classical Chinese. However, in the Meiji era a large number of new SJ-words was created to cater to the needs of a modern vocabulary, and the balance moved radically towards the SJ-words. In contemporary Japan, the amount of words in each group depends on the type of language used. The lowest percentage of SJ-words is in traditional poetry (about 5–15%), fiction for children (average about 20%), and in adult conversation on general topics (probably up to 25%). The highest percentage is found in magazines (about 40%), newspapers (45–65%), and some scientific and technical literature (up to 70% or more). In general, the more "bookish" the style, the higher the percentage of the SJ-words. L-words and mixed words together normally account for not more than 6% of all words within a particular text or conversation. This means that the number of the fully native J-words varies from approximately 90% to approximately 30% or even less.

A statistical comparison between Japanese and some European languages, for instance, French, has led to an interesting finding: it seems that in order to read a text in Japanese, we have to know a considerably larger number of words than if we read a comparable text in a European language. In other words, Japanese uses, at least in the written language, a larger variety of words than languages such as French or English. Fujio Minami has called this phenomenon "lexical extravagance" and has related it to the existence of the large number of synonyms in the language. These statistical studies support the informal observations of many foreign learners: even after years of working with the language one has to accept that words one has never seen before will be coming up on every page of a Japanese text.

Extensive synonymy is one of the special features of Japanese vocabulary. The other feature is a widespread homonymy. A concise dictionary of Japanese lists twelve different words that are all pronounced *kōsei*. In writing this does not matter, because each of the twelve words is written with completely different characters. In the spoken language this homonymy does not normally produce serious problems either: some of the words are not used with any significant frequency and others will be employed in particular compounds or expressions only; others are unambiguously distinguished by the context, such as *kōsei* (construction) and *kōsei* (proofreading).

Only a few pairs of homonyms in Japanese cause a real problem. This is true, for instance, of *kagaku* (science) and *kagaku* (chemistry), or *shiritsu* (municipal) and *shiritsu* (private). However, the Japanese have developed a way to deal with the problem. After saying *kagaku* in the meaning "chemistry" one adds: "(which could also be read) *bakegaku*." This reference to an alternative potential reading of the characters distinguishes the word from the other *kagaku*. A similar procedure is applied in the case of the word *shiritsu*. In writing the homonymy is of course fully resolved through the use of different characters.

JAPANESE WRITING

Only man could have designed a system as illogical and complicated as the Japanese system of writing. Even today, after a series of postwar reforms, the Japanese script remains the most difficult of writing systems of all languages and historical periods.

Japanese existed as only a spoken language until at least the seventh century A.D., and Chinese was used whenever it was necessary to maintain records of any kind. However, the practice of using characters phonetically to write down Japanese personal and place names and sentences or poems which had to be preserved in their original form rather than translated gradually developed. After a complex series of transformations, the *kana* syllabaries, which developed as the simplication of the shapes of characters, emerged toward the end of the first millenium. Eventually, Japanese texts came to be written down in a system combining the syllabic *kana* with characters representing certain categories of Japanese words.

Characters are thus pronounced differently in Chinese and Japanese. As far as their shapes are concerned, these remained totally identical until the postwar writing reforms in China and Japan; however, the simplification process due to these reforms meant that the shapes diverged to a considerable extent. Also, the meanings of many characters have developed differently in China and Japan. Characters that were produced in Japan (called *kokuji* in Japanese) and that do not exist in Chinese are few, but they include some very common symbols, such as the character for *hataraku* (to work) or *komu* (to be crowded). On the whole it may therefore be better to refer to characters as they are used in Japan today as "Japanese" rather than "Chinese" characters. This should in no way diminish the enormous cultural indebtedness of Japan to China, which is generally accepted by the Japanese.

Kana and Characters

The result of the historical processes is thus the existence of two kinds of symbols employed in contemporary Japanese:

1. Characters, of which approximately 3,000 to 6,000 are used in contemporary Japan; the Japanese name *kanji* is sometimes used for them.

2. *Kana,* which comprises 46 basic phonetic symbols, each representing one syllable (syllables that cannot be written with the basic symbols use diacritics or combination of symbols). There are two sets of *kana*: (a) *katakana*, the shapes of which are square and look more like parts of characters, and (b) *hiragana*, which developed from the cursive style of the characters; they have more rounded shapes than characters or *katakana*.

How is the use of these three sets of symbols differentiated? In principle, characters are used to write down the stems of most J-words as well as all SJ-words; *katakana* are employed for L-words, and *hiragana* for the rest: endings, suffixes, particles, auxiliary words, and some other words for which no characters, or only difficult characters, are available. For instance:

K K K H C C H C H H H
ジョンは化学が嫌いです
Jon wa kagaku ga kirai desu
John chemistry dislike is
"John hates chemistry"
(K = katakana, C = character, H = hiragana)

Jon is of course a loan word from English and must be written in *katakana*, as all loanwords are. *Wa* is a particle that can only be written in *hiragana*. The same is true of the particle *ga* and *desu*. *Kagaku* (chemistry) is an SJ-word composed of two elements, each corresponding to a character that—at least to some extent—indicates its meaning. The word *kirai* (dislike) is a J-word. Its stem can be written with a character, in which case the ending *-i* must be added in hiragana. Alternatively, as above, the whole word can be written in hiragana.

In other words, the writer of a Japanese text does not select just one of the three sets (characters, *hiragana*, *katakana*): all three are normally used together. There is considerable variation in usage, and many decisions—such as how to write the word *kirai* above—are left to individual writers.

The shapes of the *kana* symbols are very different from those of the Latin alphabet, but the way they are used is not basically different from our own system of writing: both are used phonetically. However, while in the alphabet each symbol (letter) stands normally for one sound, in *kana* one simple symbol nornally corresponds to a Japanese syllable (e.g., ka = か, ki = き, shi = し, etc.).

The Use of Characters

On the other hand, the use of characters is very different. In principle, each character corresponds to an element of a word with a particular meaning, or to a whole word.

Words or their elements which are pronounced in exactly the same way are represented by different characters if their meaning is different. For instance, the J-words *kawa* "river" and *kawa* "skin, leather" sound identical but they must be written with different characters because they have different meanings. The characters are 川 and 革, respectively. Should English use characters, the three homonymous words written "case" would use three different characters: (1) 箱 for case (a box), (2) 格 for case (grammatical case), and (3) 件 for case (an instance).

However, the Japanese situation is further complicated by the fact that words or elements of words which sound different, but have identical, similar, or originally identical or similar meanings, frequently use the same character. For instance, the J-word *ki* "tree, wood" and the SJ-elements *moku* and *boku*, also meaning tree, wood, use the same character, 木. Should English use characters in the same way Japanese does, the word "cat" and the element "fel-" (as in the word "feline") would probably be written with the same character, 猫.

As a result, each character in Japanese has normally one shape, a set of readings, and a set of (usually related) meanings. For instance:

Shape	Readings	Meanings
川	SEN, kawa	river
皮	HI, kawa	skin, leather
木	MOKU, BOKU, ki	tree, timber

Actually, in English the numerical symbols are used in exactly the same way as characters in Japanese:

Shape		Readings	Meanings
2	(in 32)	too	two
	(in 20)	twen	
	(in 2nd)	seco	

Some of the readings of characters are native J-words or elements of J-words. Others (those which are written in capitals in this section) are SJ-words. In Japanese, unlike in Chinese, characters with only one reading are rare. Normally there are at last two basic readings to each character, one J-reading and one SJ-reading. Some characters have more than that. 生 , one of the most commonly used characters, can be read *SEI*, *SHŌ*, *ikiru*, *umareru*, *ki*, or *nama*, with a number of variations. Among the frequent meanings of this character are "to live," "to be born," "to happen," "pure," and "raw."

In many words one wonders why a particular character and not another one, which would perfectly fit in as far as its reading and meaning are concerned, is used. Current usage, normally supported by tradition, decides. One simply has to remember that the second element in *jijō* (circumstances) is written with 情 , not with 状 , which also means "state of affairs."

When it comes to reading and writing place names and personal names, hardly any rules are followed and one must often rely on knowing that a particular reading or particular characters are employed in a particular case. In proper names characters can be used on the basis of tradition, with little reference to their usual readings. This does not create serious problems for the Japanese because they seldom have to read (i.e., to read aloud) a personal or place name they do not know—the important question for them is how to write it. However, foreigners must frequently transcribe addresses into romanization and write about Japanese people in English texts. Special dictionaries exist for the reading of proper names, but sometimes they give more than one possible reading and the most reliable method is still to find someone who knows the place or the person concerned.

Shapes of Characters

Foreigners often wonder how so many different and complicated characters can be remembered. This is actually not as difficult as one might expect.

The shape of each character consists of a relatively small number of recurring elements, graphs, which in turn consist of a very small number of acceptable "strokes." For instance, the character 河 (*KA*, *kawa* [river]), which is a synonym of the character 川 discussed above, consists of the elements 氵 and 可 both of which recur in a number of other characters.

Moreover, some of these recurring elements indicate the category of meaning which the character carries, while other elements sometimes refer to one of the readings of the character. The element 氵 used in the character 河 indicates in most characters that the meaning of the character is connected with water, liquidity, flowing, etc. For example:

池	*CHI, ike*	pond
汗	*KAN, ase*	sweat
泣	*KYŪ, naku*	to cry
浅	*SEN, asai*	shallow

However, this rule is far from being waterproof. Quite a few characters which contain the element 氵 have nothing to do with water (cf. 決 *KETSU, kimeru* [to decide]), at least not in the contemporary Japanese usage.

Readers may have wondered in what way characters are arranged in Japanese character dictionaries and here is the answer: characters which contain the element 氵, or another element of the same type, are grouped together. The 氵 group contains of course a large number of characters that are arranged within the group according to the number of strokes needed to complete them. The traditional character "alphabet" has over 200 elements such as 氵, normally referred to as radicals. To find a character in a character dictionary, one determines what its radical is, then counts the number of remaining strokes, finds the radical group in the dictionary, and finds the group of characters which need that particular number of strokes for their completion. That may be only one character, or perhaps twenty. So, it is necessary to go through all those twenty characters to find the character whose reading you are looking for. Since it is not always clear what the radical of a character is nor how to count correctly the additional number of strokes, the procedure is rather cumbersome. No wonder most native speakers prefer not to use dictionaries that are arranged according to characters. They *guess* what the reading of the character *might be* and look the word up in a different type of a dictionary arranged according to the reading of words. An alternative, practiced by many foreign speakers, is to ask a native speaker: this works for the first, say 2,000 characters, but for less frequently used ones an average native speaker may not always be a reliable source of information.

Let us return to the structure of the character 河. I have said that the left-hand element of the character, the radical, points to its meaning. The right-hand element indicates that the SJ-reading is *KA*. The same reading occurs in a considerable number of other characters containing this element:

可	*KA*	good, possibility
何	*KA, nani*	what
歌	*KA, uta*	song
苛	*KA, mugoi*	harsh

(Note, however, that the only reading of 阿 is *A*.)

Although not all characters contain a "phonetic part" such as this, most of the less frequent characters do. This is the reason the guessing strategy for looking up characters in a phonetically arranged dictionary really works.

The first and simplest characters produced in China were pictures of things, or symbols that graphically indicated relationships. In the former category one can quote the characters for sun 日, moon 月, mountain 山, river 川, etc. In the latter group belong, for instance, the characters for "up" 上, "down" 下, or "middle" 中. The character 峠 for *tōge* "a mountain pass," which was produced in Japan, is interesting. It consists of the characters for "mountain" 山, "up" 上, and "down" 下. However, it would be incorrect to assume that all or perhaps most of the Chinese characters were originally pictures of things or relationships. Most Chinese characters were produced on the basis of the "radical + phonetic part" principle. This accounts for the relative ease with which they can be remembered.

Neat Writing and Calligraphy

The shapes of printed and handwritten characters often differ in detail, so it is dangerous to study characters by simply copying them, from books or newspapers. Only one of the printing styles, that employed consistently in textbooks for lower grades of primary schools, is close to handwritten characters. However, a number of dictionaries are available for those who wish to learn how to write neatly and with the correct order of strokes.

Traditionally, Japanese was always written in vertical columns running from right to left, with pages numbered from what would be the back of a Western book. In contemporary Japan, many books, in particular textbooks and books of a technical nature, are printed in lines running in the "normal" horizontal way from left to right, with pages numbered as in European books. Personal notes and letters are also frequently written in lines. It is not necessary for a foreigner to try to be more Japanese than the Japanese themselves, and to write notes at a lecture or a letter in vertical columns.

In present-day Japan the standard writing utensils on all occasions are of course pen and pencil. However, the traditional brush is widely employed for large scale public notices and in calligraphy.

In English the word calligraphy is frequently used to describe any neat handwriting. In the Japanese context it describes a traditional art of great complexity and refinement. There are of course many schools of neat handwriting (*shūji*), but also many calligraphy (*shodō*) schools throughout Japan. Calligraphy is one of the traditional Japanese arts which are practiced by large numbers of people as a hobby. Frequent exhibitions are held.

Calligraphy can be divided into the more traditional style and the avant-garde style. Though for different reasons, both are often difficult to read without a transcription into the usual characters. To write really good calligraphy in the traditional style is a superhuman task for someone who has not been educated in Japan, but approaches to the avant-garde style may be more successful, even if less beneficial from the point of view of learning Japanese. However, to develop the ability to appreciate calligraphy is accessible to everyone and it is worth the time which needs to be invested.

WILL JAPANESE WRITING BE REFORMED?

People in the West have frequently assumed that the alphabet, and the Latin alphabet at that, represents the most advanced system of writing which can be conceived. The question, resulting from this perception, continues to be asked: when will the Japanese give up their characters and switch over to the alphabet?

The modern science of lingistics does not provide any support to those who believe that a "phonetic" alphabet is the most modern and superior system of writing. The Western alphabet developed more than two thousand years ago, ultimately from Egyptian hieroglyphs, but this happened long before any modern spirit of "rationalism" appeared. Moreover, it is interesting to realize that the medieval writing systems of Europe were mostly more "phonetic" than the contemporary spelling systems. This should be impossible were there any firm relationship between the modernization of society and the "phonetic" character of writing. Also, Japan has successfully modernized, at an accelerated rate, using its cumbersome writing system. How could the Japanese economic miracle have occurred, if the Japanese system were vastly inferior to the alphabet? Most recently, the Japanese writing system has not changed, as some expected, to enable the society to use computers. On the contrary, it was the computers that "learned" how to handle the characters.

However, it is necessary to realize that although retaining the basic principles of the writing system intact, the Japanese language did modernize under the pressure of the changing social structure, and that important changes occurred in the writing system as well.

The process of streamlining the existing system and in particular restricting and simplifying the use of characters has proceeded at a fairly even pace ever since the Meiji era. A number of radical measures were proposed at the outset of the period, and in the 1920s and early 1940s, but in view of the power of tradition and later of right-wing nationalism, none of the proposed reforms could be implemented. A great moment for the progressivists arrived after Japan's defeat in 1945. Reforms had been well prepared and the support of the Allied Occupation was at their disposal. Commencing in winter of 1946 a series of reforms was promulgated which resulted in the following changes:

1. The *kana* spelling was phoneticized. Up to that date a difficult system of *kana* spelling based on historical distinctions in pronunciation (which had long since disappeared) was in use.

2. A limit was imposed on the number of characters allowed to be used in the public sphere of life. This was the origin of the famous List of Characters for Present-Day Use (*Tōyō kanji*), comprising 1,850 characters. Up to this point no limit was imposed, and even after the 1946 reforms private use in letters, books, magazines, scientific papers, and similar texts remained unrestricted.

3. A list was prepared of readings which were allowed to be used for the *Tōyō kanji* in public use.

4. A set of characters was defined that had to be mastered by everyone during the period of compulsory education. This list of 881 Education characters is known in Japanese as *Kyōiku kanji*.

5. A special list was set up for character use in giving names to children. Of course, this list only applied in the case of newly registered given names. Previously, parents were free to select any character out of approximately 50,000 characters used at any moment in the past, either in China or in Japan.

6. The shapes of many characters were simplified.

7. An attempt was made to clearly specify which part of a word is a base (for which a character is used) and which part is a suffix or an

ending, and should therefore be written in *hiragana*. These rules are known as *okurigana* rules. Previously, the practice was not unified and, for example, the word *akiraka* (clear) could be written 明きらか (*a-kiraka*), 明らか (*aki-raka*), or 明か (*akira-ka*).

More recently some of these regulations have been revised. For example, the number of the Education Characters was raised to 996, and in 1986 a new *Jōyō kanji* list with 1,945 characters has replaced the old *Tōyō kanji* list mentioned above under (2).

On the whole, the postwar reforms were not revolutionary, but they did assist the Japanese language in a significant way in its continuing strive for rationalization. By removing a large number of characters from the public sphere of communication, they also greatly affected the vocabulary. A large number of difficult SJ-words, which had been written with abandoned characters, went out of use, and the actively used vocabulary—in particular, newly created words—was considerably simplified.

Foreign users of Japanese should of course try to follow the generally accepted usage, and this implies complying with most of the official regulations. However, it is not necessary for them to worry about what characters or readings are allowed in *Jōyō kanji*, because average Japanese speakers lack this knowledge as well. Strictly speaking, the current regulations only have the character of "guidance rules" for the public domains of communication, and do not bind individuals in their usage. The recent editions of Japanese dictionaries usually record the official usage with considerable accuracy. Also, special spelling dictionaries are readily available and will be a useful acquisition for an advanced user of Japanese.

Romanization of Japanese

In the late 1940s and in the 1950s many people overseas and quite a few in Japan expected that the postwar reforms were only the first phase of a process which would lead, in the near future, to a full romanization of Japanese. However, these expectations proved entirely false.

Proposals to abolish characters and romanize Japanese actually appeared for the first time in the Meiji era. Several systems of romanization were developed but the two that are most widely used today are the Revised Hepburn System, as used in most bilingual dictionaries of Japanese or by the Japanese Ministry of Foreign Affairs, and the Standard (*Hyōjunshiki*) system, preferred by the Ministry of Education and recently widely used in American writings about the Japanese language. In this book, the Revised Hepburn system is used.

There is, of course, no such thing as a correct romanization. Any romanization is acceptable, as long as it is consistent and easy to understand. It is certainly confusing if several systems of romanization are mixed in a haphazard way within one single sentence. Also, the use of unusual representations, such as *c* for the Hepburn *ch* or the Standard *ty*, cannot be justified in general usage, and may cause problems for the postman delivering your letter.

Anyway, the move to romanize the Japanese writing system did not succeed. Romanization is only employed in textbooks for foreigners, in writing down the names of railway stations for the convenience of foreigners, to record Japanese proper names in foreign-language texts, in headwords in Japanese-English dictionaries, and in advertizing, where it helps to emphasize the foreign origin of some products—but this is about all. There are virtually no Japanese texts written or published in romanization. Romanization is not an alternative script for the language. It has remained a convenience tool for the foreigner.

Romanization is taught in Japanese schools but competence in identifying individual words is normally all that is achieved. Even this faculty is probably more strongly supported by learning English than by learning the Japanese romanization itself. Very few people can manage to read whole sentences and still fewer can write using consistently one of the romanization systems. Even professional teachers of Japanese may find it difficult to put spaces between words in the standard way—a fact connected of course with the absence of spacing in normal Japanese texts.

Discussions in the Japanese-language teaching profession of whether it is helpful or harmful to use romanization in teaching Japanese appear again and again. Some teachers who themselves have been brought up on romanized textbooks support romanization, while some Japanese teachers, who are not familiar with romanization, are against its use. Of course, many teachers base their arguments on more sophisticated grounds. As far as learners are concerned, there are many categories. Some only wish to acquire very basic sentence patterns and vocabulary within a limited period of time, and it would be irrational to insist that they spend 20 percent of the time available on learning *kana*, which will not give them competence in reading any Japanese texts anyway. On the other hand, since the acquisition of *kana* is not really very difficult, it makes little sense to teach Japanese in romanization to students who are likely to proceed to the intermediate or advanced level. Many categories lie between these two extremes and no generally valid rules can be given for them. Let me say, however, that more important than *when* to introduce the Japanese system of writing is the fact that the system is introduced, and that it is not simply introduced but that students are intensively guided in its use. Most cases of students who started with romanization and "never later learned to use the Japanese writing" are students who were not properly required to study the Japanese writing and were not properly told how to study it.

FIVE
CONCLUSION:
WHAT TO DO?

In this book I have argued that problems in interpersonal interaction exist and that they cannot be removed simply through good will or waiting. What then should be done is a vital question. I shall close by pointing to three major avenues that may lead to a better future: an effort to understand, learning how to actually interact, and learning how to help those on the other side of the communication barrier.

HOW TO COPE

The Effort to Understand

To understand is a passive process: understanding alone does not automatically give us the competence necessary for correct behavior. For example, I may understand perfectly well that I should bow with each verbal greeting in Japanese, but to remember to do so and to execute the bow correctly requires more than simple understanding. It requires what is sometimes called "practice"; without "practice" the competence to actually perform what we "know" perfectly well cannot normally be achieved.

Understanding is thus only the first step to correct interaction. There are people who may understand problems of intercultural interaction perfectly well but will never be able to put their theoretical knowledge to practice. However, I believe that in general those who understand will become better learners and better performers. Indeed, if I did not believe so, this book would never have been written. The whole of this text is a tool for *understanding*.

To summarize, a number of general points to watch if you wish to improve your understanding of Japanese culture, communication, and language can be given. Let me suggest the following six as ones that I consider the most valuable.

Firstly, *do not search for a simple explanation of Japan through a single principle*. This approach has often been applied by both foreign and Japanese observers. A number of labels are now available, each of them claiming the power to explain the whole lot or at least large bundles of features of Japanese society: *amae*, vertical society, Zen, *tatemae* and *honne*, *oyabun-kobun* relationship, group harmony, and many others. Not that these generalizations would be nonsensical. Some of them are useful instruments that can be of interest to a student of Japan at a later stage. However, no single principle of this sort can explain as much as its proposers claim. Furthermore, at the beginners' level, such generalizing slogans can contribute to the creation of additional distance between foreigners and Japan, and as such act as brakes on the development of realistic understanding.

Secondly, *we should not succumb to the temptation to overrate differences*. Japanese society, the Japanese system of communication, and the Japanese language are basically the same as their counterparts anywhere else. Of course, there are specific features, some of them "old-fashioned," but Japan is not "unique" in this respect or in any other sense. I realize that some observers—mainly those who have been unsuccessul in penetrating the communication barrier—claim that the Japanese are mystical and irrational, that they are dishonest, hostile, or even treacherous. Of course there are irrational and dishonest people among the Japanese, as in any ethnic group in the world. However, what is needed is realism, not extreme and subjective evaluations of phenomena that may not be representative for Japanese society at all.

Thirdly, *remember that much of what you are tempted to interpret as a difference in sociocultural behavior or personality may be simply a difference in patterns of communication*. Rules of communiction, being much less universal than rules of culture, are frequently the factor responsible for Japan putting on the mask of uniqueness and inscrutability. Once the differences in communication are understood, the mask falls down and behind it appears the universal human face.

Observers of Japan have so often taken the country at its face value: what it appeared to be when the Japanese were seen communicating was accepted as what it actually was. The Japanese were emotionless because they appeared not to communicate emotions; they were excessively formal because they communicated politeness so strongly; they were cunning because they did not communicate refusal in the same way as we do. One did not ask whether they actually had emotions, whether they were actually formal, or whether they did or did not make it clear what they meant. Is it an exaggeration to say that for the average foreigner the personality of a Japanese speaker is assessed on the basis of how the Japanese appears to him through the eyes of the foreigner's *own* culture and communication?

Fourthly, *it is necessary to accept that contact situations are different from native situations.* Remember that what people do in contact situations is subject to a number of instances of rule breaking, which is not intentional or welcome, and that people in contact situations need understanding and help. They are rarely who they appear to be in contact situations.

Further, *we must always remember the importance of variation in Japanese culture, communication, and language.* There is no such thing as Japan, Japanese communication, or Japanese language as such. One of the most common failures of foreigners is the fact that they look at Japan as a single undifferentiated whole, mostly the Japan of the Tokyo middle class. However, Japan is more than that.

Finally, *every opportunity should be taken to discuss interaction problems with the Japanese, if possible not merely the Tokyo middle class.* This method is greatly underused: ask questions and make suggestions, vary situations and elicit response. While you are doing so, remember that it is difficult for everyone, not only the Japanese, to either directly or indirectly criticize other people's behavior, and that if you have your own problems in mind it will be more efficient to present them as problems of people who are unknown to your Japanese contacts. It is possible to say, for instance, "I have seen a foreigner doing this or that, what do you think that the Japanese who were looking on thought of it?" The Japanese are very often excellent partners for this purpose: frank and articulate. Of course, one can meet people who instead of their own feelings and observations will reproduce one of the stereotypes (which flourish not merely in the West but also in Japan), but isn't this what can happen everywhere? If you ask questions about particular events, the distortion will never be great. However, if your question asks the partner to summarize ("What do the Japanese think about it?"), there is more danger of the influence of stereotypic theories of Japanese society.

The position taken in this book is that Japan is a modern society, similar in its structure to any Western society. The text thus de-exoticizes Japan and the Japanese. It is doing so consciously, but not necessarily as a matter of policy: there is simply no other way. This is what Japan is. This is who the Japanese are.

Learning to Interact

Sociocultural competence   To actually learn how to behave in Japanese culture is more difficult then to simply understand it. There is some tradition of teaching how to *understand* culture, in particular, aspects of the arts, etc., but attempts to teach how to actually *interact* in a culture have only begun. Still, it is definitely important for many foreigners to learn how to conduct everyday life or how to study in Japan, or how to work in a Japanese organization. One day, and I hope this will happen soon, we will have courses that will teach not merely language or communication, but how to interact with the Japanese in general. At present, living in Japan, combined with active participation, is the only way of learning how to do things in the Japanese way. Of course, living in Japan only provides an opportunity. So many foreigners who lived in Japan in the past or who are living there at present have remained complete foreigners in the country: they have not found out what the Japanese think, how they behave in everyday life, or how they work.

The basic problem is penetration into Japanese social networks. Without membership in Japanese networks there is no participation, and without participation there is no learning. Recently, a number of organizations, even Japanese national universities, have made provision for foreigners to become full-time regular employees. Of course, the extent to which foreign employees can gain permanent membership in such networks depends on the character of the job and many other factors. However, much depends on the successful communicative adjustment of the foreigner concerned. So, in a sense, the problem of learning how to interact in Japanese culture is transposed into the problem of learning how to communicate.

Communicative competence   Again, courses which teach one to communicate—both to express one's intent and to comprehend that of others—are extemely rare. Much depends on the opportunity of foreigners to "practice." Again, participation alone, without the ability to perceive the existing similarities and differences, will be of only limited help. In the same way as with regard to culture, and perhaps more, we can meet thousands of foreigners in Tokyo and in all areas of Japan who have lived in the country for years, who perhaps speak Japanese, but who communicate in a strongly foreign way. This is not necessarily a consequence of their conscious attempt to remain foreign. To gain real communicative competence is difficult: participation in networks must go hand in hand with the deepening of understanding. In particular, since regional and social variation in communicative competence is considerable, it must be fully taken into consideration: the fact that "a Japanese" did or advised us to do something in a certain way does not automatically provide a guide to our own behavior. The prospective model may be completely unsuitable for our needs.

The need for care does not imply that communicative competence adequate for situations of contact with the Japanese cannot be achieved. Many foreigners have reached a high level of the competence in the past, and there will be more and more in the future.

One part of the system of communicative competence is the system of etiquette, and here, too, rules of behavior must be adapted to the requirements of contact situations. Members of most cultures have been led to believe that their own behavior is "natural" and correct. However, if we want to perform satisfactorily in contact situations with the Japanese we must accept that adjustments are necessary. As I have explained in Chapter Three, if we do not change, because we want to remain "ourselves," the opposite effect is achieved: we may appear to be someone else, perhaps a simple or unfriendly person we would prefer not to be.

Linguistic competence   To learn how to actually form sentences, in other words to achieve grammatical competence, is the easiest of the three tasks: there is a large selection of Japanese language courses available both overseas and in Japan. Some of them also include components of communicative competence, even if such components are generally few and remain unaccompanied by exercises.

Before starting a Japanese course do not concern yourself with tricks that would enable you to remember thousands of sentence patterns, words, or characters overnight. There are no such tricks. Besides, if you plan your study carefully, success is assured. But how should you plan for it? Let me list a few points here.

First, *it is advisable that your personal plan incorporates the study of Japanese culture and communication along with the study of Japanese language, even if such study is not included in the language course you intend to attend.* As I explained above, without the knowledge of Japan and the Japanese system of communication there can be no successful contact with Japan and the Japanese. This also means that there will be little or no opportunity to "practice," to learn.

Secondly, *always be realistic about your objectives and possibilities.* Japanese is a difficult language and for a native speaker of English it takes much more time to achieve a reasonable competence in it than, say, in French.

You can decide to study the spoken language alone. This is a legitimate aim for many categories of learners. It may also be the only target you can realistically put before yourself at the moment. It is possible to achieve considerable competence in Japanese conversation without spending much time on the script. However, you should realize that if you wish to discuss topics such as politics, economy, social problems, or literature you must also be able to read. It is difficult to acquire sufficient vocabularly unless you also study the characters. In this respect, Japanese is different from other languages.

If you wish to achieve fluency in reading you should know that very few foreigners, if any, have ever accomplished that without having taken at least a full university major in Japanese (normally not less than three years of hard work) or a well-designed intensive course (at least ten months).

Further, *select your courses carefully.* Languages are taught in many different ways. Some courses of Japanese may be too elementary, others may be too difficult. There are programs which only include the study of the written language, and others which only teach basic grammar and simple conversation. If a course devotes five hours weekly to reading of texts and only one hour to conversation you can be sure that it will never provide you with speaking competence.

Tapes and the language laboratory are an important aid. However, the teaching of conversation in a small group by an experienced teacher will contribute much more to your ability to use Japanese in natural settings than hours spent in a language laboratory.

The number of characters taught in a course usually indicates how far you will get in your reading competence. Since you cannot commence independent reading before you know approximately 1,200 to 1,500 characters, you can easily judge for youself that a course which only introduces 600 will not "get you there."

Fourthly, *classroom work is not sufficient if you wish to do really well.* Whether you live overseas or in Japan, apart from attending courses you will be well advised to develop a pattern of independent self-instruction. Unless you have developed this faculty by the time you finish your last course, you will be unable to further improve on your own.

Some of the techniques you should master are:

— using textbooks that are not prescribed for your course,
— occasional listening to radio/television broadcasts or conversation in Japanese for language acquisition (rather than for content),
— independent reading with the help of a dictionary,
— reading of books about Japanese grammar, communication, and society,
— asking native speakers of Japanese about correct Japanese usage.

You should establish contact and make friends with as many native speakers of Japanese as you can. Do not forget that you also must give in this relationship if you wish to take.

If you are in Japan, you should not forget that just simply to be there helps only very little. You must really plan your work and stick with your plan. The experience of many foreigners who lived in Japan after completing advanced courses in Japanese is that they come back to their home country and know fewer characters than when they left. Wherever possible, it is advisable to attend advanced reading classes in which someone else plans your work and checks your progress.

Finally, *develop techniques for constant monitoring and correction of your usage*. This is an extrememly important point. The acquisition of most learners "fossilizes" at a relatively low level of competence. This happens when they do not listen to their own speech critically and do not try to improve. You cannot expect that native speakers, even if asked, will correct you. To correct adults is almost impossible in any culture, not only in Japan.

Your Japanese teacher will correct some of your mistakes but not all. Record your own speech periodically and you will find that you can detect many of your problems yourself. Whenever you are in doubt, present your problems for consideration to your teacher or your Japanese friends. In any case, accept that your Japanese will not be perfect for some time to come. It will be necessary to improve it again and again, at least until the moment your Japanese friends drop the compliment customarily addressed to foreigners who are still struggling with the language: *Watashitachi yori o-jōzu desu ne!* (You speak better Japanese than we do!)

Considering the Problems of the Japanese When Communicating in English

In order to make interaction in contact situations successful, it is not sufficient to think of the non-Japanese participants alone. When communication is conducted in English, and this admittedly is the majority of contact situations involving Japanese speakers, problems of Japanese speakers need careful attention. One important point is to understand the problems, another is to develop the competence to help.

With regard to the first task it is vital to develop the ability to understand that people are not necessarily what they appear to be in contact situations. Those who appear shy may not be shy at all, while the "aggressive" ones may turn into very normal persons when they communicate in Japanese. It is a good exercise to observe how the Japanese with whom you communicate in English change when they speak to other Japanese in their own language. The change of "personality" may be quite astounding.

The most popular explanation of people's behavior in contact situations is through interference of their native system of culture: they transfer their own rules into the situations of intercultural contact. As I explained repeatedly in Chapter Three, this does happen.

However, this principle alone cannot lead to a real understanding of what is happening. Apart from interference there is the problem of incomplete and incorrect learning. Participants believe that *this* is how people behave in a foreign culture. For example, many young Japanese academics believe that in an English-speaking academic discussion everyone can openly criticize everyone else. It may be true that in America, Britain, or Australia some forms of criticism occur more easily than at a Japanese meeting, but in general constraints on criticism are many, and it is far from correct to believe that participants are free to openly criticize anyone. Another reason that deviations from English norms of behavior appear is what I referred to earlier in this book as "simplification": participants lose the ability to control the rules which in their own culture and in the target culture may be identical. For instance, when they speak in English, Japanese participants may lose the ability to control their facial expression or body movements in the way expected from them in any culture. They may laugh excessively, not because they would always laugh excessively in Japanese or because they believe that to laugh excessively is correct behavior in English, but because they just lose the competence to control their laughter. I knew a Japanese lady who was nervously lifting up one leg whenever she spoke English, whereas her manners in Japanese were absolutely perfect.

If we learn to understand, and not to rush into making judgments about the personality or real intentions of our Japanese friends on the basis of their overt behavior in contact situations, we may profit in another way: we may gradually come to realize that most of the problems they encounter in English are also present in our own behavior when we communicate in Japanese, and this may be the first step to our own improvement.

Understanding can and should lead to help. We can help our partners to understand, but we can also help in actual behavior. The latter can happen, for instance, when we accept their deviance, do not mark it negatively, and allow them to be different.

At an overseas college a number of new staff members and visitors arrived every year. In order to make them and their spouses feel comfortable it was an accepted practice to organize a party for them. However, the Japanese arrivals usually hated the party. At that time —this was in the late 1960s—parties of the American type were very unusual in Japan. As I suggested in Chapter Three, a party is a communicatively very complex structure: there are complicated rules governing the situation (entry, greetings, introductions, selection of conversation topics, change of conversation partners, distribution of drinks, table manners, departure routines, etc.). Participants who have not mastered the party rules find it difficult to behave in a way that would be satisfactory for themselves and evaluate their performance negatively. Those who do not have the competence to monitor their behavior are lucky. The more the participant knows (but cannot perform), the less happy he or she is. Some of the Japanese participants knew very little about the relevant norms and enjoyed the party. Others knew quite a lot and suffered: even when their grammatical competence in English was more or less adequate, they were not sure how to exchange greetings, how to select proper topics, how to select drinks (what is "dry sherry"?), how to refuse drinks, how to change conversation partners, or how to leave. The topics they produced were mainly comparisons of various phenomena in Japan with similar phenomena in the country they were visiting; they drank too much because they didn't know how to say "No, thank you"; they spoke only to those who came and directly addressed them; and they stayed until everyone else left, because they didn't know how to leave in a proper manner.

Rather than ask these people to come to a large party, it would have been more considerate of the organizers to invite them to participate in a smaller dinner group—say, four people, including the guests—which would function as one network (i.e., not a network split into dyads). The Japanese participants would have appreciated being able to sit down rather than to circulate (and speak up to people who were much taller than they were), to be close to other speakers (this improves the audibility of the spoken word), to be able to discuss "contact" topics (i.e., topics about Japan), and to develop a relationship of a more lasting character than can be achieved in casually speaking to a large number of people.

There will be many Japanese who do not need similar help. However, think about those who do, and be prepared to make concessions rather than to require them from others.

The term "foreigner talk" was used in Chapter Four to refer to the simplification of speech addressed to a foreign speaker. Many English speakers feel that it is degrading and impolite to address someone in simplified language. Other English speakers are prepared to use a very strong version of foreigner talk whenever they detect any kind of lack of comprehension. Both approaches are incorrect. Some Japanese speakers whose competence in English is very low will appreciate it if you simplify your language to a reasonable degree. On the other hand, they may feel uncomfortable if the simplification is too strong, if you shout at them instead of using the normal volume of your voice, or when you obviously simplify not merely the words but also the intellectual level of your conversation.

It is not only the other person who is the different one. In a contact situation we all are different. We all should help one another. It would be a very monotonous and boring world if all people were the same. Let us retain our differences and learn how to solve problems that may arise from them in contact situations.

BIBLIOGRAPHICAL
NOTES

The following notes may be of use to readers who wish to undertake further reading or are interested in the sources of facts and opinions presented in this book. They are limited to literature available in English and do not aim at exhaustiveness.

Abbreviations Used

JATJ   *Journal of the Association of Teachers of Japanese* (originally, Journal-Newsletter of the Association of Teachers of Japanese)

EOJ   Kodansha's *Encyclopedia of Japan*

LJS   *Language in Japanese Society,* ed. by F. C. C. Peng (Tokyo: University of Tokyo Press, 1975)

Proc. S.   *Proceedings of the Symposium on Japanese Sociolinguistics.* San Antonio: Trinity University 1978.

PSAL   *Post-Structural Approaches to Language—Language Theory in a Japanese Context,* by J. V. Neustupný (Tokyo: University of Tokyo Press, 1978)

Chapter I

One of the first publications on **interaction problems** between the Japanese and foreigners was *In Search of Identity* by J. W. Bennett, J.

Passin, and R. K. McKnight (The University of Minnesota Press, 1958). The book analyzed attitudes and interaction problems of Japanese students in the USA. An extensive recent survey of interaction problems between the Japanese and Westerners by S. Ramsey and J. Birk has appeared in Vol. III of the *Handbook of Intercultural Training,* edited by D. Landis and R. W. Brislin (Pergamon Press, 1983). O. Mizutani's *Japanese: The Spoken Language in Japanese Life* (The Japan Times, 1981) will be particularly useful to those readers who wish to concentrate on the communicative aspects of the interaction problem. The last chapter of *Explorations in Japanese Sociolinguistics* by L. Loveday (John Benjamins, 1986) contains a good survey of some more recent research on the topic.

Each of these publications reflects a particular view of Japan and of interaction problems, and some of those views—understandably—are not identical with those advocated in this book.

The concept and model of **communicative competence** as described here is derived from Dell Hymes' work; see his *Foundations in Sociolinguistics,* (University of Pennsylvania Press, 1974, and "On Communicative Competence," of which excerpts have been printed in *Sociolinguistics,* ed. by J. B. Pride and J. Holmes (Penguin Books, 1972).

The model of **language problems** used here derives from the author's "An Outline of the Theory of Language Problems" (PSAL, Chapter XII). Its most recent application to contact situations can be found in my contribution to *Cross-Cultural Encounters: Communication and Miscommunication,* ed. by J. B. Pride (River Seine Publications, 1985). See also B. H. Jernudd's and E. Thuan's paper in the *International Journal of the Sociology of Language* 44, 1983.

Chapter II

A large number of books about **Japanese culture and society** are available on the market, but not all of them present a neutral and realistic picture of Japan, void of stereotypic generalizations. Chie Nakane's *Japanese Society* (Penguin Books, 1973) has been widely used as an introductory text for many years, but it has also been criticized for too much emphasis on differences between Japan and the West, on the hierarchical arrangement of Japanese society, and for portraying Japan as a unique society governed by rigid and unchangeable principles. E. F. Vogel's bestseller *Japan as Number One* (Harvard University Press, 1979) attempts to identify features of Japan from which America could take a lesson. Although it provides a useful counterweight to older accounts of Japan, which could see nothing positive in the country, the resulting picture is unrealistically rosy. Anthropological introductions to Japan include Harumi Befu's excellent *Japan: An Anthropological Introduction* (Chandler, 1971). Although the book does not fully cover contemporary life of the population of large cities such as Tokyo or Osaka, it will contribute facts and interpretations that are not immediately available to a foreign observer whose experience is limited to these areas.

Any general reader will profit from the realistic portrait of Japan by the Japanese sociologist Rokuro Hidaka as presented in *The Price of Affluence* (Kodansha International, 1984, and Penguin Books 1985). Takeo Kuwabara's *Japan and Western Civilization* (University of Tokyo Press, 1983) records some unconventional attitudes toward traditional and modern Japanese culture, and Shunsuke Tsurumi's *Cultural History of Postwar Japan* (Kegan Paul International, 1987) can be recommended particularly for its treatment of Japanese popular culture. For those who are not afraid of a harder academic idiom, *Images of Japanese Society* by R. Mouer and Y. Sugimoto (Kegan Paul International, 1986) is a must. This compendium of facts and interpretations of contemporary Japanese society is free of stereotyped and exoticizing interpretations of the country. The book also contains an extensive bibliography on all aspects of contemporary Japan.

The only encyclopedic work on Japan available in English is the *Encyclopedia of Japan* (9 vols., Kodansha, 1983). The reader can be referred to this work for a second opinion on most sections of this chapter, and also for a bibliography for further reading. It should be noted here that my section on the Japanese family has drawn on A. Fuse's article in *The Japan Foundation Newsletter* 12, 1984 and on F. Kumagai's unpublished manuscript, "The Dual Structure of the Japanese Family."

Chapter III

The main source of data for Chapter III is research by my colleagues and students on various aspects of communication problems in Australian-Japanese contact situations. This work includes the following: T. Asaoka, *Behavioral Patterns and Perceived Interactional Difficulties of Australian Tourists in Japan* (M.A. thesis, 1985); T. Asaoka, "Communication Problems Between Japanese and Australians at a Dinner Party" (*Working Papers of the JSC* 3, 1987); M.A. Bolitho, "Communicative Problems in Japanese Women in Melbourne" (in *Linguistic Communications* 15, 1975); M.A. Bolitho, "Communicative Networks of Japanese Women in Melbourne" (in *Australia Talks,* ed. by M. G. Clyne, 1976); L. J. Kehoe, *Patterns of Second Language Acquisition in Japanese* (M.A. thesis, 1980); M. Kubota, *Language Problems of Japanese Children in Melbourne* (M.A. thesis, 1982); H. E. Marriott, *Acquisition of Communicative Competence by Japanese Women* (M.A. thesis, 1979), H. E. Marriott, "Written Networks among Japanese Women In Melbourne" (in *ITL* 49-50, 1980); H. E. Marriott, *English of Japanese Women In Melbourne* (*Papers of the JSC* 12, 1984); H. E. Marriott, "Introductions in Australian-Japanese Contact Situations" (*Working Papers of the JSC* 4, 1985); H. Masumi-So, *Loanwords in Melbourne Japanese* (M.A. thesis, 1983); A. Murie, *Communication Problems in Australia-Japan Business Relations* (B.A. Honours dissertation, 1976); A. Ozaki, "Requests for Clarification: A Study of Correction Strategies" (*Working Papers of the JSC* 2, 1985); A. Ozaki, *Conversational Analysis of Foreign Speakers of Japanese* (Ph.D. thesis, 1986); A. Skoutarides, *Foreigner Talk in Japanese* (Ph.D. thesis, 1986); R. L. Spence-Brown, *Japanese Exchange Students in Australia* (M.A. thesis, 1986); and K. Yoshimitsu, *Some Aspects of Communication within a Melbourne Branch of a Japanese Trading Company* (M.A. thesis, 1986). Examples have been borrowed from some of these papers. [All dissertations and theses mentioned in this paragraph have been submitted to the Department of Japanese, Monash University, Melbourne.]

Many books and papers dealing with **Japanese sociolinguistics** are of relevance to the issues discussed in this book and have been consulted.

The treatment of more than individual aspects of Japanese sociolinguistics are available in: *LJS* (1975); J. Hinds' *Aspects of Japanese Discourse Structure* (Kaitakusha, 1976); *Proc.S.* (1978); *PSAL* (1978); M. Mizutani's *Japanese: The Spoken Language in Japanese Life* (The

Japan Times, 1981); T. Suzuki's *Japanese and the Japanese* (Kodansha, 1978); a special issue of the *Journal of Pragmatics* 10, No. 3 (1986); and L. Loveday's *Explorations in Japanese Sociolinguistics* (John Benjamins, 1986).

A summary of Japanese accounts of regional **variation** in Japanese can be found in R. A. Miller's *The Japanese Language* (University of Chicago Press, 1967). Six volumes of the *Linguistic Atlas of Japan* (National Language Research Institute, 1967–74) is an exciting work for those with a serious interest in the geographical distribution of speech in Japan (*see also* Tokugawa and Kato's introductory paper in *Orbis* 15, 1966 and Grootaers and Shibata's comments in *Lingua* 57, 1982). Problems of the standardization of Japanese receive attention in K. Nomoto's (*LJS*) and T. Shibata's (*Proc.S.*) detailed studies. The question of female/male language has been discussed by E. H. Jorden in *Report of the Second U.S.-Japan Joint Sociolinguistic Conference* and in *EOJ* under "Feminine language" and "Masculine language." *See also* S. Ide's papers in *Proc.S.* and in *Lingua* 57, 1982 and J. S. Shibamoto's *Japanese Women's Language* (Academic Press, 1985). For information on other aspects of variation in Japanese, see: J. J. Chew's paper on Japanese baby talk (*JATJ* 6, 1969); A. Skoutarides' thesis on foreigner talk (quoted above); and S. Nagara's book on *Japanese Pidgin English in Hawaii* (University of Hawaii Press, 1972).

On **English** words in Japanese Masanori Higa's work (in *LJS*) should be consulted. English in Japan has received the most extensive treatment in *The Teaching of English in Japan,* ed. by I. Koike and others (Eichosha, 1978). English spoken by the Japanese overseas has first been studied by S. Ervin-Tripp (in *Journal of Social Issues* 23, 1967). For work undertaken at Monash University (Asaoka, Kehoe, Marriott, and Skoutarides) see above. Many other studies are now available on the acquisition of English by Japanese children.

The question of **address and reference** in Japanese and the use of pronouns, kinship terms, names, and other similar devices has been researched extensively, for instance by Befu and Norbeck (*Southwestern Journal of Anthropology* 14, 1958); Fischer (*American Anthropologist* 66, Part II, 1964); Passin (*Monumenta Nipponica* 21, 1966); Peng and others, in *LJS;* Hinds, in *Aspects of Japanese Discourse Structure* (Kaitakusha, 1976); and in a number of papers by Takao Suzuki (*see* his *Japanese and the Japanese,* Kodansha, 1978).

Japanese **non-verbal behavior** has received attention in S. Ishii's paper in *Communication* 2, 1973 and in H. Morsbach's contribution to *The Journal of Nervous and Mental Disease* 157, 1973. Among more recent papers dealing specifically with Japanese non-verbal behavior one can cite H. M. Taylor's research (*JATJ* 9, 1974 and *Linguistic Communications* 15, 1975) as well as Ramsey's paper on the kinesics of Japanese women (*Language Sciences* 3, 1981).

Japanese **greetings** have been discussed by Mizutani in *Proceedings of the Symposium on Japanese Language Teaching* (Trinity University, 1978) and F. Coulmas in *Conversational Routines* (Mouton, 1981). The Mizutanis' *Nihongo Notes* (6 vols, The Japan Times 1977–   ) should not escape the attention of any reader who is seeking information for both theoretical or practical purposes.

Literature on Japanese **honorifics** available in English is extensive. The relationship between politeness in Japanese and other languages of the world has been explored by the author in *PSAL*. The best practical account is the Mizutanis' *How to be Polite in Japanese* (The Japan Times, 1987). The reader is also advised to consult A. M. Niyekawa's article "Honorifics" in *EOJ*.

More factual information on postwar **Japanese language reforms** can be found in J. J. Daniels' paper available in *JATJ* 13, 1978, and in the present writer's article "Japanese Language Reforms" in *EOJ*.

Japanese **attitudes to language** have recently been discussed in a number of emotional writings by R. A. Miller (e.g., *Japan's Modern Myth,* Weatherhill, 1982). His claims lack objectivity. E. H. Jorden's paper (in *Proc.S.*) provides data from a survey. However, B. Saint-Jaques (*The Japan Foundation Newsletter* 11, 1983) gives evidence that leads to different conclusions and should also be given appropriate attention.

A number of issues of **Japanese etiquette** have been discussed in H. Befu's "An Ethnography of Dinner Entertainment in Japan" (*Arctic Anthropology* 11, 1974). A good practical introduction to Japanese etiquette is D. Rowland's *Japanese Business Etiquette* (Warner Books, 1985). Two older handbooks of Japanese etiquette for native situations are *Japanese Etiquette—An Introduction* (C. E. Tuttle, 1955) and B. Nakajima's *Japanese Etiquette* (Japan Travel Bureau, 1955).

Chapters IV and V

The best survey of the Japanese language can be found in W. Grootaers' entry in the *EOJ* entitled "Japanese language." R. A. Miller's *The Japanese Language* (University of Chicago Press, 1967) may satisfy a reader who is oriented toward historical linguistics. The most extensive grammar of contemporary Japanese published in a Western language is *A Reference Grammar of Japanese* by S. E. Martin (Yale University Press, 1975). An excellent handbook of Japanese grammar has been published by S. Makino and M. Tsutsui under the title *A Dictionary of Basic Japanese Grammar* (The Japan Times, 19867).

A large number of **textbooks** is available on the market. Some older textbooks, such as those by N. Naganuma or O. Vaccari should be avoided. Most books cover only the elementary stage, but course texts which guide the student from the very beginning up to the advanced stage are available. Students who wish to undertake much of their study independently are advised to use books which contain extensive and reliable information on Japanese grammar. This can be, for instance, Nobuko and Osamu Mizutani's *Modern Japanese* (The Japan Times), E. H. Jorden's *Beginning Japanese* (Yale University Press), or H. D. B. Clarke and M. Hamamura's *Colloquial Japanese* (Routledge and Kegan Paul, 1981).

An introduction to **Japanese script** is often included in textbooks of Japanese. The best specialized text is E. H. Jorden and H. I. Chaplin's *Reading Japanese* (Yale University Press, 1976). *See also* the present author's *Introduction to Japanese Writing* (Melbourne: Japanese Studies Centre, 1984).

Dictionaries are a problem. There is no good and extensive dictionary of Japanese that can be used by foreign users. However, *Basic Japanese-English Dictionary* compiled by The Japan Foundation (Bonjinsha 1986) is an excellent reference for the first 2,800 words. Thematically arranged vocabulary lists of limited extension can also be useful for beginners. J. V. Neustupný's *Basic Japanese Vocabulary* (Melbourne: Japanese Studies Centre, 1985) contains approximately 2,000 words. A. Seton, N. Matsumoto and N. Hayashi's *Japanese Vocabulary for Speakers and Readers* (Hokuseido Press, 1984) consists of almost 6,000 entries.

INDEX

215